ROWAN Babies

Over thirty designs for babies
and children up to five years old

Kim Hargreaves

ROWAN

Copyright © Rowan Yarns 2003
First published in Great Britain in 2003 by
Rowan Yarns Ltd
Green Lane Mill
Holmfirth
West Yorkshire
England
HD9 2DX

Internet: www.knitrowan.com
Email: rowanbabies@knitrowan.com

Designs & Styling Kim Hargreaves
Photographer Joey Toller
Hair & Make-up Mark Thomson
Models Amelia, Natasha, Gracie, Cameron, Ayana, Dalila, Ben, Morgan,
Cheyenne, Isaac, Alana, Dwight, Makoto, Mia, Dillon, Katie, Henry
Book Design Kim Hargreaves
Design Co-ordinator Stella Smith
Design Layout Les Dunford
Knitting co-ordinators Elizabeth Armitage & Michelle Moorhouse
Pattern writers Kathleen Hargreaves & Sue Whiting

British Library Cataloguing in Publication Data
Rowan Yarns
Rowan Babies
1. Knitting - patterns
1 Title
ISBN 1-904485-01-4

Printed by Fulcrum Colour Printers
Ripponden

Contents

Cotton Candy in Denim, pattern on page 71

Opposite Daydream
in Cotton Glace,
pattern page 68,
this page Relish
in Wool Cotton,
pattern page 50

Bob knitted in All Seasons Cotton, pattern page 67

Hallow knitted in All Season Cotton, pattern page 65

Duel in All Seasons Cotton, pattern page 60

Opposite Strawberry Bud in 4ply Cotton, pattern page 62,
this page Truelove in 4ply Soft, pattern page 49

Maytime in
4ply Cotton,
pattern page 54

This page Polka Dots in 4ply Cotton, pattern page 56,
opposite Lola in All Seasons Cotton, pattern page 69

Solo in Denim, pattern page 66

Opposite Wink
in Kidsilk Haze,
pattern page 51,
this page Cindy
in Cork,
pattern page 55

Cindy in Cork, pattern page 55

This page Sweeten in 4ply Soft, pattern page 72,
opposite Tranquil in 4ply Soft & Kidsilk Haze, pattern page 73

This page Dapple in All Seasons Cotton, pattern page 53,
opposite Little Trees in Wool Cotton, pattern page 70

Hans in Wool Cotton, pattern page 59

Dumpling in Big Wool, pattern page 75

This page Bo, pattern page 57 & Rupert, pattern page 76, both in Wool Cotton,
opposite Archie, pattern page 63 & Snug, pattern page 61, both in 4ply Soft

This page Holly
in Wool Cotton,
pattern page 46,
opposite Streamer
in 4ply Soft,
pattern page 74

Fame in
Big Wool,
pattern
page 48

Opposite Bo
in Wool Cotton
pattern page 57
& Snug in 4ply Soft,
pattern page 61,
this page Marshall
in Wool Cotton,
pattern page 58

Opposite Snuffle pattern page 69,
this page Husky pattern page 64, both in Big Wool

This page Docker
pattern page 74,
opposite Buster
pattern page 52,
both in Wool Cotton

THE KNITTING PATTERNS

The designs in this book are all sized according to Kim's original design and are graded accordingly. All of the garments are photographed on the correct size child; to help you to decide which size to knit we have numbered the sizes throughout the magazine to help you translate garments with the correct fit onto your child. To make this easier, there is a size diagram included with each pattern which shows not only the finished garment length and width but will also enable you to calculate the crucial centre-back to cuff measurement needed to ensure a perfect fit.

DESIGN NUMBER 1

HOLLY

YARN

	3rd	4th	5th	size
To fit age	1-2	2-3	4-5	years
To fit chest	51	56	61	cm
	20	22	24	in

Rowan Wool Cotton

A Rich	911	4	5	6 x 50gm
B Antique	900	1	1	1 x 50gm

NEEDLES

1 pair 3¼mm (no 10) (US 3) needles
1 pair 4mm (no 8) (US 6) needles

BUTTONS – 5 x 75321

TENSION

22 sts and 30 rows to 10 cm measured over stocking stitch using 4mm (US 6) needles.

BACK

Cast on 59 (65: 71) sts using 3¼mm (US 3) needles and yarn A.
Work in garter st for 8 rows, ending with a WS row.

Change to 4mm (US 6) needles.
Using the **fairisle** technique as described on the information page and starting and ending rows as indicated, work 12 rows in patt from chart for border, which is worked entirely in st st beg with a K row.
Break off yarn B and cont using yarn A only. Beg with a K row, work in st st until back measures 14 (17: 21) cm, ending with a WS row.

Shape armholes

Cast off 4 sts at beg of next 2 rows.
51 (57: 63) sts.
Cont straight until armhole measures 7 (8: 8) cm, ending with a WS row.
Using the **fairisle** technique as described on the information page and starting and ending rows as indicated, work 14 rows in patt from chart for yoke, which is worked entirely in st st beg with a K row.
Break off yarn B and cont using yarn A only.
Cont straight until armhole measures 13 (14: 15) cm, ending with a WS row.

Shape shoulders and back neck

Cast off 6 (6: 7) sts at beg of next 2 rows.
39 (45: 49) sts.
Next row (RS): Cast off 6 (6: 7) sts, K until there are 9 (11: 11) sts on right needle and turn, leaving rem sts on a holder.
Work each side of neck separately.
Cast off 4 sts at beg of next row.
Cast off rem 5 (7: 7) sts.
With RS facing, rejoin yarn to rem sts, cast off centre 9 (11: 13) sts, K to end.
Complete to match first side, reversing shapings.

LEFT FRONT

Cast on 35 (38: 41) sts using 3¼mm (US 3) needles and yarn A.

Girls version only

Work in garter st for 7 rows, ending with a RS row.

Boys version only

Work in garter st for 4 rows, ending with a WS row.
Row 5 (RS): K to last 3 sts, yfwd, K2tog (to make a buttonhole), K1.
Work in garter st for a further 2 rows, ending with a RS row.

Both versions

Row 8 (WS): K6 and slip these 6 sts onto a holder, M1, K to end. 30 (33: 36) sts.
Change to 4mm (US 6) needles.

Starting and ending rows as indicated, work 12 rows in patt from chart for border.
Break off yarn B and cont using yarn A only.
Beg with a K row, work in st st until left front measures 9 (10: 14) cm, ending with a WS row.
Place chart
Using the **intarsia** method as described on the information page, place chart for left front as folls:
Next row (RS): K4 (7: 9), work next 24 sts as row 1 of chart for left front, K to end.
Next row: P2 (2: 3), work next 24 sts as row 2 of chart for left front, P to end.
These 2 rows set position of chart.
Keeping chart correct, cont straight until left front matches back to beg of armhole shaping, ending with a WS row.

Shape armhole

Keeping chart correct, cast off 4 sts at beg of next row. 26 (29: 32) sts.
Cont straight until all 24 rows of chart have been completed, ending with a WS row.
Break off yarn B and cont using yarn A only.
Cont straight until 4 rows less have been worked than on back to start of yoke chart, ending with a WS row.

Shape front slope

Dec 1 st at end of next and foll alt row.
24 (27: 30) sts.
Work 1 row, ending with a WS row.
Starting and ending rows as indicated, work 14 rows in patt from chart for yoke and at same time dec 1 st at end of next and every foll alt row. 17 (20: 23) sts.
Break off yarn B and cont using yarn A only.

4th and 5th sizes only

Dec 1 st at end of next and foll – (0: 1) alt row.
– (19: 21) sts.

All sizes

Cont straight until left front matches back to start of shoulder shaping, ending with a WS row.

Shape shoulder

Cast off 6 (6: 7) sts at beg of next and foll alt row.
Work 1 row.
Cast off rem 5 (7: 7) sts.

RIGHT FRONT

Cast on 35 (38: 41) sts using 3¼mm (US 3) needles and yarn A.

Girls version only

Work in garter st for 4 rows, ending with a WS row.

Row 5 (RS): K1, K2tog, yfwd (to make a buttonhole), K to end.

Work in garter st for a further 2 rows, ending with a RS row.

Boys version only

Work in garter st for 7 rows, ending with a RS row.

Both versions

Row 8 (WS): K to last 6 sts, M1 and turn, leaving last 6 sts on a holder. 30 (33: 36) sts.

Change to 4mm (US 6) needles.

Starting and ending rows as indicated, work 12 rows in patt from chart for border.

Break off yarn B and cont using yarn A only.

Beg with a K row, work in st st until right front measures 9 (10: 14) cm, ending with a WS row.

Place chart

Using the **intarsia** method as described on the information page, place chart for right front as folls:

Next row (RS): K2 (2: 3), work next 24 sts as row 1 of chart for right front, K to end.

Next row: P4 (7: 9), work next 24 sts as row 2 of chart for right front, P to end.

These 2 rows set position of chart.

Keeping chart correct, complete to match left front, reversing shapings.

SLEEVES (both alike)

Cast on 37 (39: 41) sts using 3¼mm (US 3) needles and yarn A.

Work in garter st for 8 rows, ending with a WS row.

Change to 4mm (US 6) needles.

Starting and ending rows as indicated, work 12 rows in patt from chart for border and at same time inc 1 st at each end of 3rd and foll 6th row. 41 (43: 45) sts.

Break off yarn B and cont using yarn A only.

Beg with a K row, cont in st st, shaping sides by inc 1 st at each end of 3rd and every foll 4th (6th: 6th) row to 57 (59: 65) sts, then on every foll - (4th: -) row until there are - (61: -) sts.

Cont straight until sleeve measures 20 (26: 30) cm, ending with a WS row.

Cast off.

MAKING UP

PRESS as described on the information page.

Join both shoulder seams using back stitch, or mattress st if preferred.

Button band and collar

Girls version only

Slip 6 sts from left front holder onto 3¼mm (US 3) needles and rejoin yarn A with RS facing.

Boys version only

Slip 6 sts from right front holder onto 3¼mm (US 3) needles and rejoin yarn A with WS facing.

Both versions

Cont in garter st until band, when slightly stretched, fits up front opening edge to start of front slope shaping, ending at inner edge (edge that will be sewn to front).

Shape for collar

Inc 1 st at inner edge of next 19 rows, then on every foll alt row until there are 30 sts.

Cont straight until collar, unstretched, fits up front slope and across to centre back neck, ending at inner edge.

Cast off 7 sts at beg of next and foll 2 alt rows.

Work 1 row.

Cast off rem 9 sts.

Slip stitch button band in place. Mark positions for 5 buttons on this band – first to come level

with buttonhole already worked in other front, last to come 1.5 cm below start of front slope shaping and rem 3 buttons evenly spaced between.

Buttonhole band and collar

Girls version only

Slip 6 sts from right front holder onto 3¼mm (US 3) needles and rejoin yarn A with WS facing.

Boys version only

Slip 6 sts from left front holder onto 3¼mm (US 3) needles and rejoin yarn A with RS facing.

Both versions

Work to match button band and collar, reversing shapings and with the addition of a further 4 buttonholes worked to correspond with positions marked for buttons as folls:

Girls version only

Buttonhole row (RS): K1, K2tog, yfwd (to make a buttonhole), K3.

Boys version only

Buttonhole row (RS): K3, yfwd, K2tog (to make a buttonhole), K1.

Join cast-off ends of collar, then slip stitch bands and collar in place.

See information page for finishing instructions, setting in sleeves using the square set-in method.

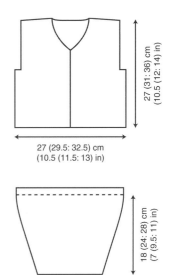

27 (31: 36) cm
(10.5 (12: 14) in)

27 (29.5: 32.5) cm
(10.5 (11.5: 13) in)

18 (24: 28) cm
(7 (9.5: 11) in)

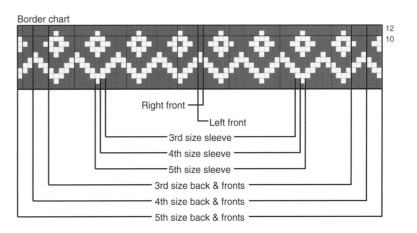

Border chart

Right front
Left front
3rd size sleeve
4th size sleeve
5th size sleeve
3rd size back & fronts
4th size back & fronts
5th size back & fronts

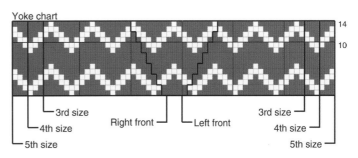

Yoke chart

3rd size
4th size
5th size
Right front
Left front
3rd size
4th size
5th size

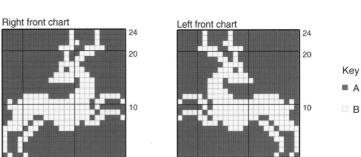

Right front chart

Left front chart

Key

■ A

☐ B

47

FAME

YARN

	3rd	4th	5th	size
To fit age	1-2	2-3	4-5	years
To fit chest	51	56	61	cm
	20	22	24	in

Rowan Big Wool

	5	6	6	x 100gm

(photographed in Arctic 013)

NEEDLES

1 pair 12mm (US 17) needles

TENSION

8 sts and 12 rows to 10 cm measured over stocking stitch using 12mm (US 17) needles.

Pattern note: As row end edges form actual finished front opening edges of garment, it is important these edges are kept neat. Therefore avoid joining in new balls of yarn at these edges.

BACK

Cast on 31 (33: 35) sts using 12mm (US 17) needles.
★★Row 1 (RS): Knit.
Row 2: P to last st, pick up loop lying between needles and place loop on right needle (**note**: this loop does NOT count as a st), sl last st purlwise.
Row 3: K tog tbl first st and the loop, K to last st, pick up loop lying between needles and place loop on right needle (**note**: this loop does NOT count as a st), sl last st knitwise.
Row 4: P tog first st and the loop, P to last st, pick up loop lying between needles and place loop on right needle, sl last st purlwise.
Last 2 rows set the slip st edging and st st.
Cont as set for a further 6 rows, ending with a WS row.★★
Beg with a K row, cont in st st across all sts as folls:
Work straight until back measures 27 (31: 37) cm, ending with a WS row.
Shape raglan armholes
Cast off 2 sts at beg of next 2 rows. 27 (29: 31) sts.
3rd and 4th sizes
Next row (RS): K1, K2tog, K to last 3 sts, K2tog tbl, K1.

Next row: P1, P2tog tbl, P to last 3 sts, P2tog, P1.
Rep last 2 rows 1 (0: -) times more. 19 (25: -) sts.
All sizes
Next row (RS): K1, K2tog, K to last 3 sts, K2tog tbl, K1.
Next row: Purl.
Rep last 2 rows 4 (6: 8) times more. 9 (11: 13) sts.
Next row (RS): K1, K2tog, K to last 3 sts, K2tog tbl, K1.
Next row: P1, P2tog tbl, P to last 3 sts, P2tog, P1.
Cast off rem 5 (7: 9) sts.

POCKET LININGS (make 2)

Cast on 8 (9: 10) sts using 12mm (US 17) needles.
Beg with a K row, work in st st for 9 (11: 13) rows, ending with a RS row.
Break yarn and leave sts on a holder.

LEFT FRONT

Cast on 17 (18: 19) sts using 12mm (US 17) needles.
Work as given for back from ★★ to ★★.
Now working side seam edge st in st st but continuing to work slip st edging up front opening edge, cont as folls:
Work straight until left front measures 12 (16: 20) cm, ending with a WS row.
Place pocket
Next row (RS): K4, cast off next 8 (9: 10) sts, patt to end.
Next row: Patt 5 sts, P across 8 (9: 10) sts of first pocket lining, P to end.
Cont straight until left front matches back to beg of raglan armhole shaping, ending with a WS row.
Shape raglan armhole
Cast off 2 sts at beg of next row. 15 (16: 17) sts.
Work 1 row.
Working all raglan decreases as given for back, dec 1 st at raglan armhole edge of next 5 (3: 1) rows, then on every foll alt row until 5 (6: 7) sts rem, then on foll row, ending with a WS row.
Break yarn and leave rem 4 (5: 6) sts on a holder.

RIGHT FRONT

Cast on 17 (18: 19) sts using 12mm (US 17) needles.
Work as given for back from ★★ to ★★.
Now working side seam edge st in st st but continuing to work slip st edging up front opening edge, cont as folls:
Work straight until right front measures 12 (16: 20) cm, ending with a WS row.
Place pocket
Next row (RS): Patt 5 sts, cast off next 8 (9: 10) sts, K to end.
Next row: P4, P across 8 (9: 10) sts of second pocket lining, patt to end.
Complete to match left front, reversing shapings.
When right front is complete, do NOT break yarn but set this ball of yarn to one side – it will be used for collar.

SLEEVES (both alike)

Cast on 15 (17: 19) sts using 12mm (US 17) needles.
Beg with a K row, cont in st st, shaping sides by inc 1 st at each end of 3rd (5th: 5th) and every foll 4th (4th: 6th) row until there are 25 (27: 29) sts.
Cont straight until sleeve measures 19 (25: 29) cm, ending with a WS row.

Shape raglan
Cast off 2 sts at beg of next 2 rows. 21 (23: 25) sts.
Working all raglan decreases as given for back, dec 1 st at each end of next and foll 4th row, then on every foll alt row until 7 sts rem.
Work 1 row, ending with a WS row.
Cast off.

MAKING UP

PRESS as described on the information page.
Join raglan seams using back stitch, or mattress st if preferred.
Collar
With RS facing and using 12mm (US 17) needles, keeping slip st edging correct and using ball of yarn set aside with right front, patt 4 (5: 6) sts from right front holder, pick up and knit 8 sts from right sleeve, 5 (7: 9) sts from back, and 8 sts from left sleeve, then patt 4 (5: 6) sts from left front holder. 29 (33: 37) sts.
Beg with a P row, cont in st st with slip st edging for a further 8 (9: 10) cm.
Cast off.
See information page for finishing instructions, leaving side seams open for first 10 rows. Make 2 twisted cords, each approx 40 cm long, and attach to front opening edges level with beg of raglan armhole shaping to form ties.

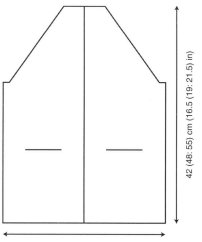

39 (41.5: 44) cm (15.5 (16.5: 17.5) in)

42 (48: 55) cm (16.5 (19: 21.5) in)

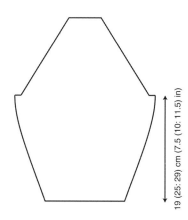

19 (25: 29) cm (7.5 (10: 11.5) in)

Truelove

YARN

	1st	2nd	3rd	4th	5th	size
	months		years			
To fit age	0-6	6-12	1-2	2-3	4-5	
To fit chest	41	46	51	56	61	cm
	16	18	20	22	24	in

Rowan 4 ply Soft

A Wink	377	2	3	3	4	5	x 50gm
B Honk	374	1	1	1	1	1	x 50gm

NEEDLES

1 pair 2³/₄mm (no 12) (US 2) needles
1 pair 3¹/₄mm (no 10) (US 3) needles
2³/₄mm (no 12) (US 2) circular needle

BUTTONS – 1 x 75315

TENSION

28 sts and 36 rows to 10 cm measured over stocking stitch using 3¹/₄mm (US 3) needles.

BACK

Cast on 281 (313: 345: 377: 409) sts using 2³/₄mm (US 2) circular needle and yarn A.
Row 1 (RS): K1, *K2, lift first of these 2 sts over 2nd st and off right needle, rep from * to end.
Row 2: P1, *P2tog, rep from * to end.
71 (79: 87: 95: 103) sts.
Change to 3¹/₄mm (US 3) needles.
Beg with a K row, cont in st st until back measures 13 (16: 19: 22: 26) cm, ending with a WS row.
Shape raglan armholes
Cast off 5 sts at beg of next 2 rows.
61 (69: 77: 85: 93) sts.
Next row (RS): K1, K2tog, K to last 3 sts, K2tog tbl, K1.
Next row: P1, P2tog tbl, P to last 3 sts, P2tog, P1.
Working all raglan decreases as set by last 2 rows, dec 1 st at each end of next 3 (5: 7: 9: 11) rows, then on every foll alt row until 43 (45: 47: 49: 51) sts rem.
Work 1 row, ending with a WS row.
Divide for back opening
Next row (RS): K1, K2tog, K18 (19: 20: 21: 22) and turn, leaving rem sts on a holder.
20 (21: 22: 23: 24) sts.

Work each side of neck separately.
Dec 1 st at raglan armhole edge of 2nd and every foll alt row until 11 (12: 13: 14: 15) sts rem, then on foll row, ending with a WS row.
Cast off rem 10 (11: 12: 13: 14) sts.
With RS facing, rejoin yarn to rem sts, K2tog, K to last 3 sts, K2tog tbl, K1. 20 (21: 22: 23: 24) sts.
Complete to match first side, reversing shapings.

FRONT

Work as given for back until 8 (8: 6: 4: 2) rows less have been worked than on back to beg of raglan armhole shaping, ending with a WS row.

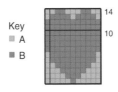

Key
■ A
■ B

Place chart
Using the **intarsia** method as described on the information page, place chart as folls:
Next row (RS): K30 (34: 38: 42: 46), work next 11 sts as row 1 of chart, K to end.
Next row: P30 (34: 38: 42: 46), work next 11 sts as row 2 of chart, P to end.
These 2 rows set position of chart.
Keeping chart correct, cont as folls:
Work 6 (6: 4: 2: 0) rows, ending with a WS row.
Shape raglan armholes
Cast off 5 sts at beg of next 2 rows.
61 (69: 77: 85: 93) sts.
Working all raglan decreases as given for back, dec 1 st at each end of next 4 (4: 6: 8: 10) rows, completing all 14 rows of chart and ending with a WS row. 53 (61: 65: 69: 73) sts.
Completing front using yarn A only, cont as folls:
Dec 1 st at each end of next 1 (3: 3: 3: 3) rows, then on every foll alt row until 33 (35: 39: 41: 43) sts rem.
Work 1 row, ending with a WS row.
Shape neck
Next row (RS): K1, K2tog, K6 (6: 8: 8: 8) and turn, leaving rem sts on a holder.
8 (8: 10: 10: 10) sts.
Work each side of neck separately.
Dec 1 st at neck edge of next 3 (3: 4: 4: 4) rows **and at same time** dec 1 st at raglan armhole edge of 2nd and foll 0 (0: 1: 1: 1) alt row. 4 sts.
Work 0 (0: 1: 1: 1) row, ending with a WS row.
Next row (RS): K1, K3tog.
Next row: P2.
Next row: K2tog and fasten off.
With RS facing, rejoin yarn to rem sts, cast off centre 15 (17: 17: 19: 21) sts, K to last 3 sts, K2tog tbl, K1. 8 (8: 10: 10: 10) sts.
Complete to match first side, reversing shapings.

SLEEVES

Cast on 153 (161: 169: 177: 185) sts using 2³/₄mm (US 2) circular needle and yarn A.
Row 1 (RS): K1, *K2, lift first of these 2 sts over 2nd st and off right needle, rep from * to end.
Row 2: P1, *P2tog, rep from * to end.
39 (41: 43: 45: 47) sts.
Change to 3¹/₄mm (US 3) needles.
Beg with a K row, cont in st st, shaping sides by inc 1 st at each end of 3rd (5th: 5th: 5th: 7th) and every foll alt (4th: 4th: 6th: 6th) row to

47 (63: 61: 71: 69) sts, then on every foll 4th (-: 6th: -: 8th) row until there are 59 (-: 67: -: 75) sts.
Cont straight until sleeve measures 13 (16: 20: 26: 30) cm, ending with a WS row.
Shape raglan
Cast off 5 sts at beg of next 2 rows.
49 (53: 57: 61: 65) sts.
Working all raglan decreases as given for back, dec 1 st at each end of next 5 (5: 3: 3: 3) rows, then on every foll alt row until 15 (15: 17: 17: 17) sts rem.
Work 1 row, ending with a WS row.
Left sleeve only
Dec 1 st at each end of next row.
13 (13: 15: 15: 15) sts.
Cast off 4 sts at beg of next row.
9 (9: 11: 11: 11) sts.
Dec 1 st at beg of next row, then cast off 4 (4: 5: 5: 5) sts at beg of foll row.
Right sleeve only
Cast off 5 sts at beg and dec 1 st at end of next row. 9 (9: 11: 11: 11) sts.
Work 1 row.
Cast off 4 (4: 5: 5: 5) sts at beg and dec 1 st at end of next row.
Work 1 row.
Both sleeves
Cast off rem 4 (4: 5: 5: 5) sts.

MAKING UP

PRESS as described on the information page.
Join raglan seams using back stitch, or mattress st if preferred.
Back opening edging
With RS facing, using 2³/₄mm (US 2) needles and yarn A, pick up and knit 18 sts down right side of back opening, then 18 sts up left side of back opening. 36 sts.
Cast off knitwise (on WS).
Neckband
With RS facing, using 2³/₄mm (US 2) circular needle and yarn A, starting and ending at back opening edges, pick up and knit 10 (11: 12: 13: 14) sts from left back neck, 11 (11: 13: 13: 13) sts from left sleeve, 5 (5: 7: 7: 7) sts down left side of neck, 15 (17: 17: 19: 21) sts from front, 5 (5: 7: 7: 7) sts up right side of neck, 11 (11: 13: 13: 13) sts from right sleeve, then 10 (11: 12: 13: 14) sts from right back neck. 67 (71: 81: 85: 89) sts.
Beg with a K row, work in rev st st for 4 rows.
Cast off knitwise (on WS).
See information page for finishing instructions.
Make a buttonloop and attach button to fasten back neck opening.

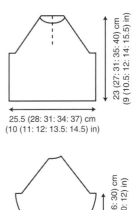

25.5 (28: 31: 34: 37) cm
(10 (11: 12: 13.5: 14.5) in)

23 (27: 31: 35: 40) cm
(9 (10.5: 12: 14: 15.5) in)

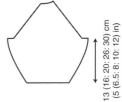

13 (16: 20: 26: 30) cm
(5 (6.5: 8: 10: 12) in)

Relish

YARN

	1st	2nd	3rd	4th	5th	size
	months		years			
To fit age	0-6	6-12	1-2	2-3	4-5	
To fit chest	41	46	51	56	61	cm
	16	18	20	22	24	in

Rowan Wool Cotton

| | 2 | 3 | 4 | 4 | 5 x 50gm |

(photographed in Hiss 952)

NEEDLES

1 pair 3¼mm (no 10) (US 3) needles
1 pair 4mm (no 8) (US 6) needles

TENSION

22 sts and 30 rows to 10 cm measured over stocking stitch using 4mm (US 6) needles.

SPECIAL ABBREVIATIONS

Fringe 1 = Cast on 5 sts, then cast off these 5 sts – one extra st now on right needle.

BACK

Cast on 45 (51: 57: 63: 69) sts using 3¼mm (US 3) needles.
Rows 1 and 2: Knit.
Row 3: K2 (1: 4: 3: 2), ★fringe 1, K3, rep from ★ to last 3 (2: 5: 4: 3) sts, fringe 1, K2 (1: 4: 3: 2).
Row 4: K2 (1: 4: 3: 2), ★P1, K3, rep from ★ to last 3 (2: 5: 4: 3) sts, P1, K2 (1: 4: 3: 2).
Rows 5 and 6: Knit.
Row 7: K4 (3: 2: 1: 4), ★fringe 1, K3, rep from ★ to last 5 (4: 3: 2: 5) sts, fringe 1, K4 (3: 2: 1: 4).
Row 8: K4 (3: 2: 1: 4), ★P1, K3, rep from ★ to last 5 (4: 3: 2: 5) sts, P1, K4 (3: 2: 1: 4).
Rep last 8 rows once more, ending with a WS row.
Change to 4mm (US 6) needles.
Beg with a K row, cont in st st until back measures 11 (13: 17: 19: 23) cm, ending with a WS row.
Shape raglan armholes
Cast off 4 sts at beg of next 2 rows.
37 (43: 49: 55: 61) sts.
Next row (RS): K1, K2tog, K to last 3 sts, K2tog tbl, K1.
Working all raglan decreases as set by last row, dec 1 st at each end of 4th and every foll 4th

row to 27 (35: 43: 51: 59) sts, then on every foll alt row until 13 (15: 17: 19: 21) sts rem.
Work 1 row, ending with a WS row.
Cast off.

LEFT FRONT

Cast on 23 (26: 29: 32: 35) sts using 3¼mm (US 3) needles.
Rows 1 and 2: Knit.
Row 3: K2 (1: 4: 3: 2), ★fringe 1, K3, rep from ★ to last st, K1.
Row 4: K4, ★P1, K3, rep from ★ to last 3 (2: 5: 4: 3) sts, P1, K2 (1: 4: 3: 2).
Rows 5 and 6: Knit.
Row 7: K4 (3: 2: 1: 4), ★fringe 1, K3, rep from ★ to last 3 sts, fringe 1, K2.
Row 8: K2, ★P1, K3, rep from ★ to last 5 (4: 3: 2: 5) sts, P1, K4 (3: 2: 1: 4).
Rep last 8 rows once more, ending with a WS row.
Change to 4mm (US 6) needles.
Beg with a K row, cont in st st until left front matches back to beg of raglan armhole shaping, ending with a WS row.
Shape raglan armhole
Cast off 4 sts at beg of next row.
19 (22: 25: 28: 31) sts.
Work 1 row.
Work all raglan decreases as given for back, dec 1 st at raglan armhole edge of next and every foll – (4th: 4th: 4th: 4th) row until 18 (20: 23: 25: 29) sts rem.
5th size only
Dec 1 st at raglan armhole edge of 2nd and foll 2 alt rows. 26 sts.
All sizes
Work 3 (1: 3: 1: 1) rows, ending with a WS row.
Shape front slope
Dec 1 st at front slope edge of next and foll 4 (5: 2: 10: 10) alt rows **and at same time** dec 1 st at raglan armhole edge of next (3rd: next: next: next) and every foll 4th (4th: 4th: alt: alt) row. 10 (11: 18: 3: 4) sts.
1st size
Dec 1 st at each end of 4th and foll 4th row. 6 sts.
1st, 2nd and 3rd sizes
Dec 1 st at raglan armhole edge of 2nd and foll 1 (4: 7: –: –) alt rows **and at same time** dec 1 st at front slope edge of 4th (2nd: 2nd: –: –) and foll 0 (0: 5: –: –) alt rows, then on every foll 0 (4th: 4th: –: –) row. 3 (3: 3: 3: 4) sts.
All sizes
Next row (WS): Purl.
Next row: K1, (K2tog) 1 (1: 1: 1: 0) times, (K3tog) 0 (0: 0: 0: 1) times. 2 sts.
Next row: P2.
Next row: K2tog and fasten off.

RIGHT FRONT

Cast on 23 (26: 29: 32: 35) sts using 3¼mm (US 3) needles.
Rows 1 and 2: Knit.
Row 3: K4, ★fringe 1, K3, rep from ★ to last 3 (2: 5: 4: 3) sts, fringe 1, K2 (1: 4: 3: 2).
Row 4: K2 (1: 4: 3: 2), ★P1, K3, rep from ★ to last st, K1.
Rows 5 and 6: Knit.
Row 7: K2, ★fringe 1, K3, rep from ★ to last 5 (4: 3: 2: 5) sts, fringe 1, K4 (3: 2: 1: 4).
Row 8: K4 (3: 2: 1: 4), ★P1, K3, rep from ★ to last 3 sts, P1, K2.
Rep last 8 rows once more, ending with a WS row.
Change to 4mm (US 6) needles.
Complete to match left front, reversing shapings.

SLEEVES

Cast on 31 (33: 35: 37: 39) sts using 3¼mm (US 3) needles.
Rows 1 and 2: Knit.
Row 3: K1 (2: 1: 2: 1), ★fringe 1, K3, rep from ★ to last 2 (3: 2: 3: 2) sts, fringe 1, K1 (2: 1: 2: 1).
Row 4: K1 (2: 1: 2: 1), ★P1, K3, rep from ★ to last 2 (3: 2: 3: 2) sts, P1, K1 (2: 1: 2: 1).
Rows 5 and 6: Knit.
Row 7: K3 (4: 3: 4: 3), ★fringe 1, K3, rep from ★ to last 0 (1: 0: 1: 0) st, K0 (1: 0: 1: 0).
Row 8: K3 (4: 3: 4: 3), ★P1, K3, rep from ★ to last 0 (1: 0: 1: 0) st, K0 (1: 0: 1: 0).
These 8 rows form fringe patt.
Cont in fringe patt, inc 1 st at each end of next and foll 4th (4th: 6th: 0: 0) row.
35 (37: 39: 39: 41) sts.
Work a further 3 (3: 1: 7: 7) rows, ending with a WS row. (16 rows of fringe patt completed.)
Change to 4mm (US 6) needles.
Beg with a K row, cont in st st, shaping sides by inc 1 st at each end of next (next: 5th: next: 3rd) and every foll 4th (4th: 6th: 8th: 8th) row to 39 (51: 45: 47: 57) sts, then on every foll alt (–: 4th: 6th: –) row until there are 49 (–: 53: 55: –) sts.
Cont straight until sleeve measures 12 (15: 19: 25: 29) cm, ending with a WS row.
Shape raglan
Cast off 4 sts at beg of next 2 rows.
41 (43: 45: 47: 49) sts.
Working all raglan decreases as given for back, dec 1 st at each end of next and foll 4th row, then on every foll alt row until 15 sts rem.
Work 1 row, ending with a WS row.
Left sleeve only
Dec 1 st at each end of next row. 13 sts.
Cast off 2 sts at beg of next row. 11 sts.
Dec 1 st at beg of next row, then cast off 3 sts at beg of foll row. 7 sts.
Rep last 2 rows once more.
Right sleeve only
Cast off 3 sts at beg and dec 1 st at end of next row. 11 sts.
Work 1 row.
Rep last 2 rows twice more.
Both sleeves
Cast off rem 3 sts.

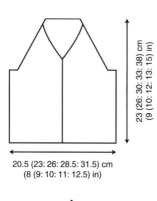

23 (26: 30: 33: 38) cm
(9 (10: 12: 13: 15) in)

20.5 (23: 26: 28.5: 31.5) cm
(8 (9: 10: 11: 12.5) in)

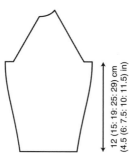

12 (15: 19: 25: 29) cm
(4.5 (6: 7.5: 10: 11.5) in)

MAKING UP

PRESS as described on the information page.
Join raglan seams using back stitch, or mattress st if preferred.

Front band

With RS facing and using 3¼mm (US 3) needles, starting and ending at cast-on edges, pick up and knit 29 (35: 45: 51: 61) sts up right front opening edge to start of front slope shaping, 20 sts up right front slope, 9 sts from right sleeve, 13 (15: 17: 19: 21) sts from back neck, 9 sts from left sleeve, 20 sts down left front slope to start of front slope shaping, then 29 (35: 45: 51: 61) sts down left front opening edge.

129 (143: 165: 179: 201) sts.
Beg with a K row, work in rev st st for 3 rows.
Cast off purlwise.
See information page for finishing instructions.
Make 2 twisted cords, each approx 20 cm long, and attach to inside of front opening edges to form ties.

DESIGN NUMBER 5

WINK

YARN

	3rd	4th	5th	size
To fit age	1-2	2-3	4-5	years
To fit chest	51	56	61	cm
	20	22	24	in

Rowan Kidsilk Haze

	4	5	6	x 25gm

(photographed in Dewberry 600)

NEEDLES

1 pair 3mm (no 11) (US 2/3) needles
1 pair 3¼mm (no 10) (US 3) needles
1 pair 3¾mm (no 9) (US 5) needles

BUTTONS – 3 x 75322

TENSION

23 sts and 32 rows to 10 cm measured over stocking stitch using 3¾mm (US 5) needles and yarn DOUBLE.

Note: Yarn is used DOUBLE throughout.

BACK

Cast on 83 (89: 95) sts using 3mm (US 2/3) needles and yarn DOUBLE.
Row 1 (RS): K0 (1: 0), P0 (2: 1), ★K3, P2, rep from ★ to last 3 (1: 4) sts, K3 (1: 3), P0 (0: 1).
Row 2: P0 (1: 0), K0 (2: 1), ★P3, K2, rep from ★ to last 3 (1: 4) sts, P3 (1: 3), K0 (0: 1).
These 2 rows form rib.
Work in rib for a further 8 rows, ending with a WS row.

Change to 3¾mm (US 5) needles.
Beg with a K row, cont in st st until back measures 19 (22: 26) cm, ending with a WS row.
Shape armholes
Cast off 4 sts at beg of next 2 rows. 75 (81: 87) sts.
Dec 1 st at each end of next 3 rows.
69 (75: 81) sts.★★
Cont straight until armhole measures 11 (12: 13) cm, ending with a WS row.
Divide for back opening
Next row (RS): K34 (37: 40) and turn, leaving rem sts on a holder.
Work each side of neck separately.
Cont straight until armhole measures 16 (17: 18) cm, ending with a WS row.
Shape shoulder and back neck
Cast off 7 (7: 8) sts at beg of next row, then 10 (11: 12) sts at beg of foll row. 17 (19: 20) sts.
Cast off 7 (7: 8) sts at beg of next row, then 4 sts at beg of foll row.
Cast off rem 6 (8: 8) sts.
With RS facing, rejoin yarn to rem sts, K2tog, K to end.
Complete to match first side, reversing shapings.

FRONT

Work as given for back to ★★.
Cont straight until 12 rows less have been worked than on back to start of shoulder shaping, ending with a WS row.
Shape neck
Next row (RS): K28 (30: 32) and turn, leaving rem sts on a holder.
Work each side of neck separately.
Dec 1 st at neck edge of next 6 rows, then on foll 2 alt rows. 20 (22: 24) sts.
Work 1 row, ending with a WS row.
Shape shoulder
Cast off 7 (7: 8) sts at beg of next and foll alt row.
Work 1 row.
Cast off rem 6 (8: 8) sts.
With RS facing, rejoin yarn to rem sts, cast off centre 13 (15: 17) sts, K to end.
Complete to match first side, reversing shapings.

SLEEVES (both alike)

Cast on 43 (45: 47) sts using 3mm (US 2/3) needles and yarn DOUBLE.
Row 1 (RS): Knit.
Row 2: K1, ★(P1, yrn, P1, yrn, P1) all into next st, K1, rep from ★ to end.
Row 3: Purl.
Row 4: K1, ★sl 2, P3tog, p2sso, K1; rep from ★ to end.
Row 5: Knit.
Row 6: K2, ★(P1, yrn, P1, yrn, P1) all into next st, K1, rep from ★ to last st, K1.
Row 7: Purl.
Row 8: K2, ★sl 2, P3tog, p2sso, K1; rep from ★ to last st, K1.

These 8 rows form bobble patt.
Work in bobble patt for a further 4 rows, inc 1 st at each end of 3rd of these rows and ending with a WS row. 45 (47: 49) sts.
Change to 3¾mm (US 5) needles.
Beg with a K row, cont in st st, shaping sides by inc 1 st at each end of 3rd (3rd: 5th) and every foll 4th row to 57 (73: 83) sts, then on every foll alt (alt: -) row until there are 75 (79: -) sts.
Cont straight until sleeve measures 19 (25: 29) cm, ending with a WS row.
Shape top
Cast off 4 sts at beg of next 2 rows. 67 (71: 75) sts.
Dec 1 st at each end of next and foll 2 alt rows.
Work 1 row, ending with a WS row.
Cast off rem 61 (65: 69) sts.

MAKING UP

PRESS as described on the information page.
Join shoulder seams using back stitch, or mattress st if preferred.

Collar

Cast on 91 (95: 99) sts using 3¼mm (US 3) needles and yarn DOUBLE.
Beg with a K row, work in st st for 5 (6: 6) cm, ending with a WS row.
Beg with row 1, work in bobble patt as given for sleeves until collar measures 10 (12: 12) cm, ending after patt row 4 or 8.
Knit 1 row. Cast off **loosely** knitwise (on WS).
Matching ends of collar to back opening edges, sew cast-on edge of collar to neck edge so that when collar is folded over RS of bobble patt shows. Fold collar in half at back neck and stitch in place. Make 3 button loops along back end of collar and attach buttons to opposite end to fasten back neck.
See information page for finishing instructions, setting in sleeves using the shallow set-in method.

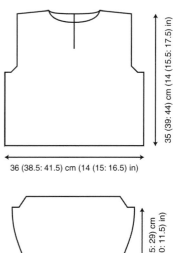

36 (38.5: 41.5) cm (14 (15: 16.5) in)

35 (39: 44) cm (14 (15.5: 17.5) in)

19 (25: 29) cm (7.5 (10: 11.5) in)

Buster

YARN

	1st	2nd	3rd	4th	5th	size
	months		years			
To fit age	0-6	6-12	1-2	2-3	4-5	
To fit chest	41	46	51	56	61	cm
	16	18	20	22	24	in

Rowan Wool Cotton

A Misty	903	2	3	3	4	4	x 50gm
B Inky	908	1	2	2	2	3	x 50gm

NEEDLES

1 pair 3¼mm (no 10) (US 3) needles
1 pair 4mm (no 8) (US 6) needles

BUTTONS – 5 x 75316

TENSION

22 sts and 30 rows to 10 cm measured over stocking stitch using 4mm (US 6) needles.

BACK

Cast on 58 (64: 70: 76: 82) sts using 3¼mm (US 3) needles and yarn A.
Row 1 (RS): K0 (0: 0: 1: 0), P2 (1: 0: 2: 2), *K2, P2, rep from * to last 0 (3: 2: 1: 0), K0 (2: 2: 1: 0), P0 (1: 0: 0: 0).
Row 2: P0 (0: 0: 1: 0), K2 (1: 0: 2: 2), *P2, K2, rep from * to last 0 (3: 2: 1: 0), P0 (2: 2: 1: 0), K0 (1: 0: 0: 0).
These 2 rows form rib.
Work in rib for a further 4 rows, ending with a WS row.
Change to 4mm (US 6) needles.
Beg with a K row, cont in st st until back measures 12 (15: 17: 20: 24) cm, ending with a WS row.
Shape raglan armholes
Cast off 4 sts at beg of next 2 rows.
50 (56: 62: 68: 74) sts.
Dec 1 st at each end of next 5 rows, then on every foll alt row until 18 (20: 22: 24: 26) sts rem, then on foll row, ending with a WS row.
Cast off rem 16 (18: 20: 22: 24) sts.

LEFT FRONT

Cast on 29 (32: 35: 38: 41) sts using 3¼mm (US 3) needles and yarn A.

Row 1 (RS): K0 (0: 0: 1: 0), P2 (1: 0: 2: 2), *K2, P2, rep from * to last 3 sts, K2, P1.
Row 2: K1, *P2, K2, rep from * to last 0 (3: 2: 1: 0), P0 (2: 2: 1: 0), K0 (1: 0: 0: 0).
These 2 rows form rib.
Work in rib for a further 4 rows, ending with a WS row.
Change to 4mm (US 6) needles.
Beg with a K row, cont in st st until 14 rows less have been worked than on back to start of raglan armhole shaping, ending with a WS row.
Place chart
Using the **intarsia** method as described on the information page, place chart as folls:
Next row (RS): K10 (12: 14: 16: 18), work next 16 sts as row 1 of chart for left front, K to end.
Next row: P3 (4: 5: 6: 7), work next 16 sts as row 2 of chart for left front, P to end.
These 2 rows set position of chart.
Keeping chart correct, work a further 12 rows, ending with a WS row.
Shape raglan armhole
Cast off 4 sts at beg of next row.
25 (28: 31: 34: 37) sts.
Work 1 row.
Dec 1 st at raglan armhole edge of next 5 rows.
20 (23: 26: 29: 32) sts.
Work 1 row, ending with a WS row. (All 22 rows of chart completed.)
Beg with a K row and using yarn A only, cont as folls:
Dec 1 st at raglan armhole edge of next and every foll alt row until 13 (14: 16: 17: 18) sts rem, ending with a RS row.
Shape neck
Cast off 6 (7: 7: 8: 9) sts at beg of next row.
7 (7: 9: 9: 9) sts.
Dec 1 st at neck edge of next 3 rows, then on foll 0 (0: 1: 1: 1) alt rows **and at same time** dec 1 st at raglan armhole edge of next and every foll alt row. 2 sts.
Work 1 row.
Next row (RS): K2tog and fasten off.

RIGHT FRONT

Cast on 29 (32: 35: 38: 41) sts using 3¼mm (US 3) needles and yarn A.
Row 1 (RS): P1, *K2, P2, rep from * to last 0 (3: 2: 1: 0), K0 (2: 2: 1: 0), P0 (1: 0: 0: 0).
Row 2: P0 (0: 0: 1: 0), K2 (1: 0: 2: 2), *P2, K2, rep from * to last 3 sts, P2, K1.
These 2 rows form rib.
Work in rib for a further 4 rows, ending with a WS row.
Change to 4mm (US 6) needles.
Beg with a K row, work in st st until 14 rows less have been worked than on back to start of raglan armhole shaping, ending with a WS row.
Place chart
Using the **intarsia** method as described on the information page, place chart as folls:
Next row (RS): K3 (4: 5: 6: 7), work next 16 sts as row 1 of chart for right front, K to end.
Next row: P10 (12: 14: 16: 18), work next 16 sts as row 2 of chart for right front, P to end.
These 2 rows set position of chart.
Complete to match left front, reversing shapings.

SLEEVES

Cast on 30 (34: 34: 38: 38) sts using 3¼mm (US 3) needles and yarn B.
Row 1 (RS): P2, *K2, P2, rep from * to end.
Row 2: K2, *P2, K2, rep from * to end.
These 2 rows form rib.
Work in rib for a further 4 rows, inc 1 st at each end of 3rd of these rows and ending with a WS row. 32 (36: 36: 40: 40) sts.
Change to 4mm (US 6) needles.
Beg with a K row, cont in st st, shaping sides by inc 1 st at each end of 3rd (3rd: 3rd: 5th: 5th) and every foll 4th (4th: 4th: 6th: 6th) row to 44 (40: 42: 46: 50) sts, then on every foll – (6th: 6th: 8th: 8th) row until there are – (48: 52: 56: 60) sts.
Cont straight until sleeve measures 12 (15: 19: 25: 29) cm, ending with a WS row.
Shape raglan
Cast off 4 sts at beg of next 2 rows.
36 (40: 44: 48: 52) sts.

Right front chart

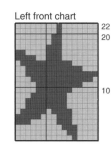

Left front chart

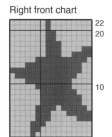

Key
 A
 B

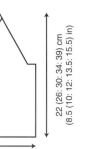

26.5 (29: 32: 34.5: 37.5) cm
(10.5 (11.5: 12.5: 13.5: 15) in)

22 (26: 30: 34: 39) cm
(8.5 (10: 12: 13.5: 15.5) in)

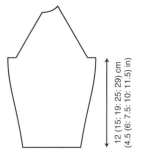

12 (15: 19: 25: 29) cm
(4.5 (6: 7.5: 10: 11.5) in)

Dec 1 st at each end of next and every foll alt row until 12 sts rem.

Work 1 row, ending with a WS row.

Left sleeve only

Dec 1 st at each end of next row. 10 sts.

Cast off 3 sts at beg of next row. 7 sts.

Dec 1 st at beg of next row, then cast off 3 sts at beg of foll row.

Right sleeve only

Cast off 4 sts at beg and dec 1 st at end of next row. 7 sts.

Work 1 row.

Cast off 3 sts at beg and dec 1 st at end of next row.

Work 1 row.

Both sleeves

Cast off rem 3 sts.

MAKING UP

PRESS as described on the information page. Join raglan seams using back stitch, or mattress st if preferred.

Button band

With RS facing, using 3¼mm (US 3) needles and yarn A, pick up and knit 42 (54: 58: 66: 78) sts along one front opening edge between neck shaping and cast-on edge.

Row 1 (WS): P2, *K2, P2, rep from * to end.

Row 2: K2, *P2, K2, rep from * to end.

Rep last 2 rows once more.

Cast off in rib.

Buttonhole band

Work to match button band, picking up sts along other front opening edge and making buttonholes in row 2 as folls:

Row 2 (RS): Rib 3, *work 2 tog, yrn (to make a buttonhole), rib 7 (10: 11: 13: 16), rep from * 3 times more, work 2 tog, yrn (to make 5th buttonhole), rib 1.

Collar

Cast on 64 (68: 76: 80: 84) sts using 3¼mm (US 3) needles and yarn A.

Row 1 (RS): K3, *P2, K2, rep from * to last st, K1.

Row 2: K1, P2, *K2, P2, rep from * to last st, K1.

Rep last 2 rows until collar measures 6 (6: 7: 7: 8) cm.

Cast off in rib.

See information page for finishing instructions. Placing ends of collar halfway across top of bands, sew cast-on edge of collar to neck edge.

DESIGN NUMBER 7

DAPPLE

YARN

	4th	5th	size
To fit age	2-3	4-5	years
To fit chest	56	61	cm
	22	24	in

Rowan All Seasons Cotton

| | 5 | 7 | x 50gm |

(photographed in Cookie 169)

NEEDLES

1 pair 4mm (no 8) (US 6) needles

1 pair 5mm (no 6) (US 8) needles

TENSION

17 sts and 24 rows to 10 cm measured over stocking stitch using 5mm (US 8) needles.

BACK

Cast on 3 sts using 5mm (US 8) needles.

Row 1 (RS): Knit.

Row 2 and every foll alt row: Purl.

Row 3: (K1, M1) twice, K1. 5 sts.

Row 5: K2, M1, K1, M1, K2. 7 sts.

Row 7: K3, yfwd, M1, K1, M1, yfwd, K3. 11 sts.

Row 9: K3, yfwd, K to last 3 sts, yfwd, K3.

Row 11: K3, yfwd, K1, M1, K to last 4 sts, M1, K1, yfwd, K3.

Row 12: Purl.★★

Rep rows 9 to 12, 17 (19) times more. 119 (131) sts.

Next row (RS): K3, yfwd, K to last 3 sts, yfwd, K3.

Next row: Purl.

Rep last 2 rows once more. 123 (135) sts.

Shape back neck

Next row (RS): K3, yfwd, K50 (55) and turn, leaving rem sts on a holder.

Work each side of neck separately.

Dec 1 st at neck edge of next row.

Break yarn and leave rem 53 (58) sts on a holder.

With RS facing, rejoin yarn to rem sts, cast off centre 17 (19) sts, K to last 3 sts, yfwd, K3.

Dec 1 st at neck edge of next row.

Break yarn and leave rem 53 (58) sts on a holder.

FRONT

Work as given for back to ★★.

Rep rows 9 to 12, 13 (15) times more. 95 (107) sts.

Next row (RS): K3, yfwd, K to last 3 sts, yfwd, K3. 97 (109) sts.

Next row: Purl.

Divide for front opening

Next row (RS): K3, yfwd, K1, M1, K44 (50) and turn, leaving rem sts on a holder.

Work each side of neck separately.

Next row (WS): Purl.

Next row: K3, yfwd, K to end.

Next row: Purl.

Next row: K3, yfwd, K1, M1, K to end.

Rep last 4 rows once more, then first of these 2 rows again, ending after a RS row. 57 (63) sts.

Shape neck

Cast off 5 (6) sts at beg of next row. 52 (57) sts.

Next row (RS): K3, yfwd, K1, M1, K to last 2 sts, K2tog.

Next row: P2tog, P to end. 52 (57) sts.

Next row: K3, yfwd, K to last 2 sts, K2tog.

Next row: Purl.

Rep last 2 rows once more. 52 (57) sts.

Next row (RS): K3, yfwd, K to end.

Next row: Purl.

Break yarn and leave rem 53 (58) sts on a holder.

With RS facing, rejoin yarn to rem sts, K2tog, K to last 4 sts, M1, K1, yfwd, K3.

Complete to match first side, reversing shapings.

MAKING UP

PRESS as described on the information page. Holding front and back WS facing, cast off sts of each shoulder/overarm edge together by taking one st from each needle together.

Front opening border

With RS facing and using 4mm (US 6) needles, pick up and knit 10 sts down left side of neck opening, place marker on needle, then pick up and knit 10 sts up right side of neck. 20 sts.

Cast off knitwise (on WS), dec 1 st at either side of marker.

Neckband

With RS facing and using 4mm (US 6) needles, starting and ending at cast-off edge of front opening border, pick up and knit 14 (15) sts up right side of neck, 19 (21) sts from back, then 14 (15) sts down left side of neck. 47 (51) sts.

Cast off knitwise (on WS).

Cut 25 cm lengths of yarn and knot groups of 4 lengths through every other eyelet hole around outer edge to form fringe. Make 2 twisted cords, each 20 cm long, and attach to ends of neck border to form ties.

See information page for finishing instructions.

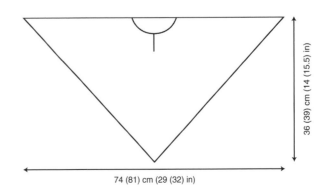

36 (39) cm (14 (15.5) in)

74 (81) cm (29 (32) in)

Maytime

YARN

	1st	2nd	3rd	4th	5th	size
	months		years			
To fit age	0-6	6-12	1-2	2-3	4-5	
To fit chest	41	46	51	56	61	cm
	16	18	20	22	24	in
Rowan 4 ply Cotton						
	2	2	3	3	4 x 50gm	

(photographed in Ripple 121)

NEEDLES

1 pair 2¾mm (no 12) (US 2) needles
1 pair 3mm (no 11) (US 2/3) needles
3mm (no 10) (US D3) crochet hook

BUTTONS – 4 x 75322

TENSION

28 sts and 38 rows to 10 cm measured over
stocking stitch using 3mm (US 2/3) needles.
One crochet motif measures 5.5 cm square.

CROCHET ABBREVIATIONS

Ss = slip stitch; **ch** = chain; **dc** = double
crochet; **htr** = half treble; **tr** = treble.

BACK

Cast on 61 (69: 77: 85: 93) sts using 2¾mm
(US 2) needles.
Beg with a K row, work in st st for 2 rows.
Change to 3mm (US 2/3) needles.
Cont in st st until back measures 5 (7: 9: 12: 16) cm,
ending with a WS row.
Shape raglan armholes
Cast off 6 sts at beg of next 2 rows.
49 (57: 65: 73: 81) sts.
1st and 2nd sizes
Next row (RS): P2, K2tog, K to last 4 sts,
K2tog tbl, P2.
Next row: K2, P to last 2 sts, K2.
Next row: P2, K to last 2 sts, P2.
Next row: K2, P to last 2 sts, K2.
Rep last 4 rows 3 (1: –: –: –) times more.
41 (53: –: –: –) sts.
4th and 5th sizes
Next row (RS): P2, K2tog, K to last 4 sts,
K2tog tbl, P2.

Next row: K2, P2tog tbl, P to last 4 sts, P2tog,
K2.
Rep last 2 rows – (–: –: 1: 3) times more.
– (–: –: 65: 65) sts.
All sizes
Next row (RS): P2, K2tog, K to last 4 sts,
K2tog tbl, P2.
Next row: K2, P to last 2 sts, K2.
Rep last 2 rows 9 (14: 19: 18: 17) times more.
21 (23: 25: 27: 29) sts.
Next row (RS): P2, K2tog, K to last 4 sts,
K2tog tbl, P2.
Next row: K2, P2tog tbl, P to last 4 sts, P2tog,
K2.
Cast off rem 17 (19: 21: 23: 25) sts.

LEFT FRONT

Cast on 31 (35: 39: 43: 47) sts using 2¾mm
(US 2) needles.
Beg with a K row, work in st st for 2 rows.
Change to 3mm (US 2/3) needles.
Cont in st st until left front matches back to beg
of raglan armhole shaping, ending with a WS
row.
Shape raglan armhole
Cast off 6 sts at beg of next row.
25 (29: 33: 37: 41) sts.
Work 1 row.
Working all raglan decreases as given for back,
cont as folls:
1st and 2nd sizes
Dec 1 st at raglan armhole edge of next and
every foll 4th row until 21 (27: –: –: –) sts rem.
Work 3 rows, ending with a WS row.
All sizes
Dec 1 st at raglan armhole edge of next 1 (1: 1:
5: 9) rows, then on every foll alt row until
16 (17: 19: 20: 21) sts rem, ending with a RS row.
Shape neck
Cast off 6 (7: 7: 8: 9) sts at beg of next row.
10 (10: 12: 12: 12) sts.
Dec 1 st at neck edge of next 4 (4: 5: 5: 5) rows
and at same time dec 1 st at raglan armhole
edge of next and every foll alt row. 4 sts.
3rd, 4th and 5th sizes
Next row (WS): P2, K2.
All sizes
Next row (RS): P1, P3tog. 2 sts.
Next row: K2.
Next row: P2tog and fasten off.

RIGHT FRONT

Work to match left front, reversing shapings.

SLEEVES

Cast on 37 (39: 41: 43: 45) sts using 2¾mm
(US 2) needles.
Beg with a K row, work in st st for 2 rows.
Change to 3mm (US 2/3) needles.
Cont in st st, shaping sides by inc 1 st at each
end of next (next: next: 3rd: 3rd) and every foll
alt (4th: 4th: 6th: 6th) row to 63 (47: 67: 57: 71) sts,
then on every foll – (alt: –: 4th: –) row until there
are – (65: –: 69: –) sts.
Cont straight until sleeve measures 9 (12: 16: 20:
24) cm, ending with a WS row.
Shape raglan
Cast off 6 sts at beg of next 2 rows.
51 (53: 55: 57: 59) sts.
Working all raglan decreases as given for back,
dec 1 st at each end of next and every foll alt
row until 19 sts rem.
Work 1 row, ending with a WS row.
Left sleeve only
Dec 1 st at each end of next row. 17 sts.

Cast off 3 sts at beg of next row. 14 sts.
Dec 1 st at beg of next row, then cast off 4 sts at
beg of foll row. 9 sts.
Rep last 2 rows once more.
Right sleeve only
Cast off 4 sts at beg and dec 1 st at end of next
row.
Work 1 row. 14 sts.
Rep last 2 rows twice more.
Both sleeves
Cast off rem 4 sts.

MAKING UP

PRESS as described on the information page.
Join raglan seams using back stitch, or mattress st
if preferred. Join side and sleeve seams.
Hem border
Using 3mm (US D3) crochet hook, make 6 ch
and join with a ss to form a ring.
Round 1: 3 ch (counts as first tr), 2 tr into ring,
(2 ch, 3 tr into ring) 3 times, 1 htr into top of
3 ch at beg of round.
Round 2: 3 ch (counts as first tr), (2 tr, 2 ch and
3 tr) into sp created by htr at end of previous
round, 2 ch, ★miss 3 tr, (3 tr, 2 ch and 3 tr into
next ch sp, rep from ★ twice more, 1 htr into top
of 3 ch at beg of round.
Round 3: 3 ch (counts as first tr), 2 tr into sp
created by htr at end of previous round, ★★2 ch,
miss 3 tr, (3 tr, 2 ch and 3 tr) into next ch sp,
2 ch★★, miss 3 tr, 3 tr into next ch sp, rep from ★
to end, ending last rep at ★★, ss to top of 3 ch at
beg of round.
Fasten off.
Make a further 7 (8: 9: 10: 11) motifs in this way,
then join motifs to form one long strip. Sew one
edge of this motif strip to lower edge of fronts
and back, matching ends of strip to front
opening edges.
Mark positions for 4 buttonholes along right
front opening edge – top buttonhole to come
just below neck cast-off, and rem 4 buttonholes
2 (2: 2.5: 2.5: 3) cm apart.
Edging
With RS facing and using 3mm (US D3)
crochet hook, rejoin yarn at lower edge of left
front opening edge and work 1 round of dc
evenly around entire hem, front opening and
neck edges, working 3 dc into each corner point
and ending with ss to first dc, **turn**.

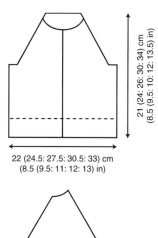

21 (24: 26: 30: 34) cm
(8.5 (9.5: 10: 12: 13.5) in)

22 (24.5: 27.5: 30.5: 33) cm
(8.5 (9.5: 11: 12: 13) in)

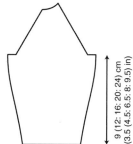

9 (12: 16: 20: 24) cm
(3.5 (4.5: 6.5: 8: 9.5) in)

Next round (WS): 1 ch (does NOT count as st), 1 dc into each dc up left front opening edge to neck corner, 1 dc into same place as last dc, ★3 ch, ss to last dc, 1 dc into each of next 3 dc, rep from ★ around neck edge to right front neck corner, 1 dc into same place as last dc, 1 dc into each dc down right front opening edge replacing (1 dc into each of next 2 dc) with (2 ch) at

positions marked for buttonholes, 1 dc into same place as last dc, ★3 ch, ss to last dc, 1 dc into each of next 3 dc, rep from ★ across lower edge, ending with ss to first dc of this round.
Fasten off.

Cuff edging
With RS facing and using 3mm (US D3) crochet hook, rejoin yarn at base of sleeve seam

and work 1 round of dc evenly around cast-on edge of sleeve.
Next round: 1 ch (does NOT count as st), 1 dc into first dc, ★3 ch, ss to last dc★★, 1 dc into each of next 3 dc, rep from ★ to end, ending last rep at ★★, 1 dc into next dc, ss to first dc.
Fasten off.
See information page for finishing instructions.

DESIGN NUMBER 9

CINDY

YARN

	1st	2nd	3rd	4th	5th	size
	months		years			
To fit age	0-6	6-12	1-2	2-3	4-5	
To fit chest	41	46	51	56	61	cm
	16	18	20	22	24	in
Rowan Cork						
	2	3	3	4	5 x 50gm	

(photographed in Chilly 32)

NEEDLES
1 pair 7mm (no 2) (US 10½) needles
1 pair 8mm (no 0) (US 11) needles
4mm (no 8) (US G6) crochet hook

BUTTONS – 1 x 75338

TENSION
14 sts and 19 rows to 10 cm measured over stocking stitch using 8mm (US 11) needles.

Tension note: Some knitters may have problems achieving the stated tension using 8mm (US 11) needles. Please ensure you take time to check your tension and adjust your needle size accordingly if required.

CROCHET ABBREVIATIONS
Ss = slip stitch; **ch** = chain.

BACK
Cast on 30 (34: 38: 42: 46) sts using 7mm (US 10½) needles.
Knit 2 rows, ending with a WS row.
Change to 8mm (US 11) needles.

Beg with a K row, cont in st st until back measures 8 (11: 14: 17: 21) cm, ending with a WS row.
Shape armholes
Cast off 4 sts at beg of next 2 rows.
22 (26: 30: 34: 38) sts.
Cont straight until armhole measures 11 (12: 13: 14: 15) cm, ending with a WS row.
Shape shoulders and back neck
4th and 5th sizes
Cast off - (-: -: 3: 4) sts at beg of next 2 rows.
- (-: -: 28: 30) sts.
All sizes
Next row (RS): Cast off 2 (3: 4: 3: 4) sts, K until there are 7 (8: 8: 8: 7) sts on right needle and turn, leaving rem sts on a holder.
Work each side of neck separately.
Cast off 4 sts at beg of next row.
Cast off rem 3 (4: 4: 4: 3) sts.
With RS facing, rejoin yarn to rem sts, cast off centre 4 (4: 6: 6: 8) sts, K to end.
Complete to match first side, reversing shapings.

LEFT FRONT
Cast on 16 (18: 20: 22: 24) sts using 7mm (US 10½) needles.
Knit 2 rows, ending with a WS row.
Change to 8mm (US 11) needles.
Beg with a K row, cont in st st until left front matches back to beg of armhole shaping, ending with a WS row.
Shape armhole
Cast off 4 sts at beg of next row.
12 (14: 16: 18: 20) sts.
Cont straight until 5 (5: 7: 7: 7) rows less have been worked than on back to start of shoulder shaping, ending with a RS row.
Shape neck
Cast off 4 (4: 4: 4: 5) sts at beg of next row.
8 (10: 12: 14: 15) sts.
Dec 1 st at neck edge of next 3 rows, then on foll 0 (0: 1: 1: 1) alt row. 5 (7: 8: 10: 11) sts.
Work 1 row, ending with a WS row.
Shape shoulder
Cast off 2 (3: 4: 3: 4) sts at beg of next and foll 0 (0: 0: 1: 1) alt row.
Work 1 row. Cast off rem 3 (4: 4: 4: 3) sts.

RIGHT FRONT
Work to match left front, reversing shapings.

SLEEVES (both alike)
Cast on 22 (22: 24: 24: 26) sts using 7mm (US 10½) needles.
Knit 2 rows, ending with a WS row.
Change to 8mm (US 11) needles.
Beg with a K row, cont in st st, shaping sides by inc 1 st at each end of 5th (3rd: 5th: 5th: 5th) and every foll 6th (4th: 6th: 6th: 6th) row to 26 (34: 30: 34: 42) sts, then on every foll 4th (-: 4th: 4th: -) row until there are 30 (-: 36: 40: -) sts.
Cont straight until sleeve measures 14.5 (17.5: 21.5: 27.5: 31.5) cm, ending with a WS row. Cast off.

MAKING UP
PRESS as described on the information page. Join both shoulder seams using back stitch, or mattress st if preferred.
Front bands (both alike)
With RS facing and using 7mm (US 10½) needles, pick up and knit 23 (29: 33: 39: 46) sts evenly along one front opening edge between cast-on edge and neck shaping.
Cast off knitwise (on WS).
Neckband
With RS facing and using 7mm (US 10½) needles, starting and ending at cast-off edge of front bands, pick up and knit 12 (12: 15: 15: 16) sts up right side of neck, 12 (12: 14: 14: 16) sts from back, then 12 (12: 15: 15: 16) sts down left side of neck. 36 (36: 44: 44: 48) sts.
Knit 2 rows.
Cast off knitwise (on WS).
Cuff edging
With RS of sleeve facing and using 4mm (G6) crochet hook, rejoin yarn to cast-on edge at right edge and work fringe as folls: ss into base of first st, ★12 ch, ss into same cast-on st★★, ss into next cast-on st, rep from ★ to end, ending last rep at ★★.
Fasten off.
Work a second row of fringing in the same way but working into sts of garter st ridge just above cast-on edge.
Hem edging
Work as given for cuff edging, working fringing across lower edge of back and fronts.
See information page for finishing instructions, setting in sleeves using the square set-in method.
Make button loop and attach button to fasten neck edge.

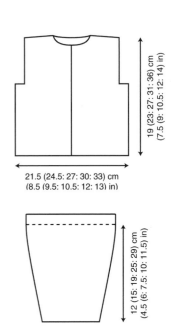

21.5 (24.5: 27: 30: 33) cm
(8.5 (9.5: 10.5: 12: 13) in)

19 (23: 27: 31: 36) cm
(7.5 (9: 10.5: 12: 14) in)

12 (15: 19: 25: 29) cm
(4.5 (6: 7.5: 10: 11.5) in)

Polka dots

YARN

	1st	2nd	3rd	4th	5th	size
	months		years			
To fit age	0-6	6-12	1-2	2-3	4-5	
To fit chest	41	46	51	56	61	cm
	16	18	20	22	24	in

Rowan 4 ply Cotton

		1st	2nd	3rd	4th	5th	
A Fresh	131	2	3	4	4	5	x 50gm
B Aegean	129	1	1	2	2	2	x 50gm
C Flirty	127	1	1	1	1	1	x 50gm

NEEDLES

1 pair 2¼mm (no 13) (US 1) needles
1 pair 3mm (no 11) (US 2/3) needles
2¼mm (no 13) (US 1) circular needle

BUTTONS – 5 x 75333

TENSION

28 sts and 38 rows to 10 cm measured over stocking stitch using 3mm (US 2/3) needles.

BACK

Cast on 289 (321: 353: 385: 417) sts using 2¼mm (US 1) circular needle and yarn C.
**Break off yarn C and join in yarn A.
Row 1 (RS): K1, *K2, lift first of these 2 sts over 2nd st and off right needle, rep from * to end.
Row 2: P1, *P2tog, rep from * to end.**
73 (81: 89: 97: 105) sts.
Change to 3mm (US 2/3) needles.
Using the **intarsia** technique as described on the information page, starting and ending rows as indicated and repeating the 40 row repeat throughout, cont in patt from chart, which is worked entirely in st st beg with a K row, as folls:
Cont straight until back measures 14 (17: 20: 23: 27) cm, ending with a WS row.
Shape armholes
Keeping patt correct, cast off 6 sts at beg of next 2 rows. 61 (69: 77: 85: 93) sts.
Cont straight until armhole measures 12 (13: 14: 15: 16) cm, ending with a WS row.
Shape shoulders and back neck
Cast off 6 (7: 8: 9: 10) sts at beg of next 2 rows. 49 (55: 61: 67: 73) sts.
Next row (RS): Cast off 6 (7: 8: 9: 10) sts, patt until there are 10 (11: 12: 13: 14) sts on right needle and turn, leaving rem sts on a holder.
Work each side of neck separately.
Cast off 4 sts at beg of next row.
Cast off rem 6 (7: 8: 9: 10) sts.
With RS facing, rejoin yarns to rem sts, cast off centre 17 (19: 21: 23: 25) sts, patt to end.
Complete to match first side, reversing shapings.

LEFT FRONT

Cast on 149 (165: 181: 197: 213) sts using 2¼mm (US 1) circular needle and yarn C.
Work edging as given for back from ** to **.
38 (42: 46: 50: 54) sts.

Change to 3mm (US 2/3) needles.
Starting and ending rows as indicated, cont in patt from chart as folls:
Cont straight until left front matches back to beg of armhole shaping, ending with a WS row.
Shape armhole
Keeping patt correct, cast off 6 sts at beg of next row. 32 (36: 40: 44: 48) sts.
Cont straight until 11 (11: 13: 13: 13) rows less have been worked on back to start of shoulder shaping, ending with a RS row.
Shape neck
Cast off 6 (7: 7: 8: 9) sts at beg of next row.
26 (29: 33: 36: 39) sts.
Dec 1 st at neck edge of next 7 rows, then on foll 1 (1: 2: 2: 2) alt rows. 18 (21: 24: 27: 30) sts.
Work 1 row, ending with a WS row.
Shape shoulder
Cast off 6 (7: 8: 9: 10) sts at beg of next and foll alt row.
Work 1 row.
Cast off rem 6 (7: 8: 9: 10) sts.

RIGHT FRONT

Work to match left front, reversing shapings.

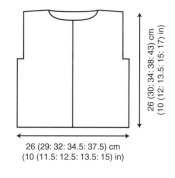

26 (30: 34: 38: 43) cm
(10 (12: 13.5: 15: 17) in)

26 (29: 32: 34.5: 37.5) cm
(10 (11.5: 12.5: 13.5: 15) in)

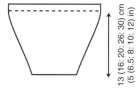

13 (16: 20: 26: 30) cm
(5 (6.5: 8: 10: 12) in)

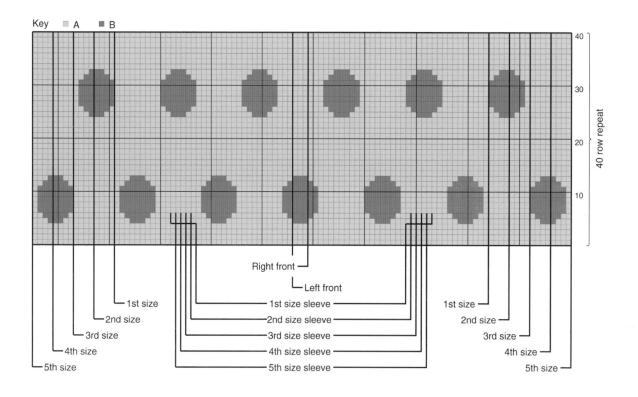

Key ☐ A ■ B

40
30
20
10

40 row repeat

Right front
Left front

1st size
2nd size
3rd size
4th size
5th size

1st size sleeve
2nd size sleeve
3rd size sleeve
4th size sleeve
5th size sleeve

1st size
2nd size
3rd size
4th size
5th size

SLEEVES (both alike)
Cast on 161 (169: 177: 185: 193) sts using 2¼mm (US 1) circular needle and yarn C.
Work edging as given for back from ★★ to ★★.
41 (43: 45: 47: 49) sts.
Change to 3mm (US 2/3) needles.
Starting and ending rows as indicated, cont in patt from chart, shaping sides by inc 1 st at each end of 5th (5th: 5th: 5th: 7th) and every foll 4th (4th: 4th: 6th: 6th) row to 55 (67: 77: 61: 69) sts, then on every foll alt (alt: alt: 4th: 4th) row until there are 67 (73: 79: 85: 91) sts, taking inc sts into patt.
Cont straight until sleeve measures 15 (18: 22: 28: 32) cm, ending with a WS row. Cast off.

MAKING UP

PRESS as described on the information page.
Join both shoulder seams using back stitch, or mattress st if preferred.
Neckband
With RS facing, using 2¼mm (US 1) needles and yarn A, starting and ending at front opening edges, pick up and knit 21 (22: 25: 26: 27) sts up right side of neck, 25 (27: 29: 31: 33) sts from back, then 21 (22: 25: 26: 27) sts down left side of neck. 67 (71: 79: 83: 87) sts.
Beg with a K row, work in rev st st for 4 rows.
Cast off knitwise (on WS).
Button band
With RS facing, using 2¼mm (US 1) needles and

yarn A, pick up and knit 66 (78: 86: 98: 114) sts down left front opening edge.
Beg with a K row, work in rev st st for 4 rows.
Cast off knitwise (on WS).
Buttonhole band
With RS facing, using 2¼mm (US 1) needles and yarn A, pick up and knit 66 (78: 86: 98: 114) sts up right front opening edge.
Row 1 (WS): Knit.
Row 2: P2, ★yrn, P2tog, P13 (16: 18: 21: 25), rep from ★ 3 times more, yrn, P2tog, P2.
Beg with a K row, work in rev st st for 2 rows.
Cast off knitwise (on WS).
See information page for finishing instructions, setting in sleeves using the square set-in method.

Bo

YARN

	1st	2nd	3rd	4th	5th	size
	months		years			
To fit age	0-6	6-12	1-2	2-3	4-5	
To fit chest	41	46	51	56	61	cm
	16	18	20	22	24	in

Rowan Wool Cotton
3   3   4   5   6 x 50gm
(photographed in Antique 900)

NEEDLES
1 pair 3¼mm (no 10) (US 3) needles
1 pair 3¾mm (no 9) (US 5) needles
1 pair 4mm (no 8) (US 6) needles

TENSION
22 sts and 30 rows to 10 cm measured over stocking stitch using 4mm (US 6) needles.

BACK
Cast on 59 (65: 71: 77: 83) sts using 3¾mm (US 5) needles.
Row 1 (RS): K1 (0: 2: 0: 0), P2 (1: 2: 2: 0), ★K3, P2, rep from ★ to last 1 (4: 2: 0: 3) sts, K1 (3: 2: 0: 3), P0 (1: 0: 0: 0).
Row 2: P1 (0: 2: 0: 0), K2 (1: 2: 2: 0), ★P3, K2, rep from ★ to last 1 (4: 2: 0: 3) sts, P1 (3: 2: 0: 3), K0 (1: 0: 0: 0).

These 2 rows form rib.
Work in rib for a further 6 rows, ending with a WS row.
Change to 4mm (US 6) needles.
Beg with a K row, cont in st st until back measures 10 (13: 16: 19: 23) cm, ending with a WS row.
Shape armholes
Cast off 5 sts at beg of next 2 rows.
49 (55: 61: 67: 73) sts.
Cont straight until armhole measures 14 (15: 16: 17: 18) cm, ending with a WS row.
Shape shoulders and back neck
Cast off 4 (5: 5: 6: 7) sts at beg of next 2 rows.
41 (45: 51: 55: 59) sts.
Next row (RS): Cast off 4 (5: 5: 6: 7) sts, K until there are 8 (8: 10: 10: 10) sts on right needle and turn, leaving rem sts on a holder.
Work each side of neck separately.
Cast off 4 sts at beg of next row.
Cast off rem 4 (4: 6: 6: 6) sts.
With RS facing, rejoin yarn to rem sts, cast off centre 17 (19: 21: 23: 25) sts, K to end.
Complete to match first side, reversing shapings.

FRONT
Work as given for back until 10 (10: 12: 12: 12) rows less have been worked than on back to start of shoulder shaping, ending with a WS row.
Shape neck
Next row (RS): K19 (21: 24: 26: 28) and turn, leaving rem sts on a holder.
Work each side of neck separately.
Dec 1 st at neck edge of next 6 rows, then on foll 1 (1: 2: 2: 2) alt rows.
12 (14: 16: 18: 20) sts.
Work 1 row, ending with a WS row.
Shape shoulder
Cast off 4 (5: 5: 6: 7) sts at beg of next and foll alt row.
Work 1 row.
Cast off rem 4 (4: 6: 6: 6) sts.
With RS facing, slip centre 11 (13: 13: 15: 17) sts onto a holder, rejoin yarn to rem sts, K to end.
Complete to match first side, reversing shapings.

SLEEVES (both alike)
Cast on 41 (43: 45: 47: 49) sts using 3¾mm (US 5) needles.
Row 1 (RS): K2 (0: 0: 0: 1), P2 (0: 1: 2: 2), ★K3, P2, rep from ★ to last 2 (3: 4: 0: 1) sts, K2 (3: 3: 0: 1), P0 (0: 1: 0: 0).
Row 2: P2 (0: 0: 0: 1), K2 (0: 1: 2: 2), ★P3, K2, rep from ★ to last 2 (3: 4: 0: 1) sts, P2 (3: 3: 0: 1), K0 (0: 1: 0: 0).
These 2 rows form rib.

Work in rib for a further 6 rows, inc 1 st at each end of 3rd of these rows and ending with a WS row. 43 (45: 47: 49: 51) sts.
Change to 4mm (US 6) needles.
Beg with a K row, cont in st st, shaping sides by inc 1 st at each end of next and every foll alt (4th: 4th: 4th: 6th) row to 63 (49: 61: 73: 59) sts, then on every foll - (alt: alt: alt: 4th) row until there are - (67: 71: 75: 79) sts.
Cont straight until sleeve measures 12 (14: 18: 22: 26) cm, ending with a WS row.
Cast off.

MAKING UP
PRESS as described on the information page.
Join right shoulder seam using back stitch, or mattress st if preferred.
Neckband
With RS facing and using 3¼mm (US 3) needles, pick up and knit 13 (14: 15: 16: 16) sts down left side of neck, knit across 11 (13: 13: 15: 17) sts from front holder, pick up and knit 13 (14: 15: 16: 16) sts up right side of neck, then 25 (26: 29: 30: 33) sts from back.
62 (67: 72: 77: 82) sts.
Row 1 (WS): K2, ★P3, K2, rep from ★ to end.
Row 2: P2, ★K3, P2, rep from ★ to end.
Rep last 2 rows twice more.
Beg with a P row, work in st st for 5 rows.
Cast off **loosely** knitwise.
See information page for finishing instructions, setting in sleeves using the square set-in method.

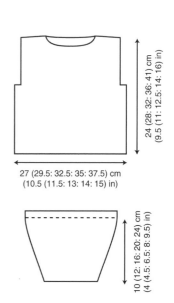

24 (28: 32: 36: 41) cm
(9.5 (11: 12.5: 14: 16) in)

27 (29.5: 32.5: 35: 37.5) cm
(10.5 (11.5: 13: 14: 15) in)

10 (12: 16: 20: 24) cm
(4 (4.5: 6.5: 8: 9.5) in)

MARSHALL

YARN

	1st	2nd	3rd	4th	5th	size
	months		years			
To fit age	0-6	6-12	1-2	2-3	4-5	
To fit chest	41	46	51	56	61	cm
	16	18	20	22	24	in

Rowan Wool Cotton

| 3 | 4 | 5 | 6 | 7 x 50gm |

(photographed in Camel 945)

NEEDLES

1 pair 3¼mm (no 10) (US 3) needles
1 pair 4mm (no 8) (US 6) needles
Cable needle

TENSION

22 sts and 30 rows to 10 cm measured over
stocking stitch using 4mm (US 6) needles.

SPECIAL ABBREVIATIONS

C4B = Cable 4 back Slip next 2 sts onto cable
needle and leave at back of work, K2, then K2
from cable needle.
C4F = Cable 4 front Slip next 2 sts onto cable
needle and leave at front of work, K2, then K2
from cable needle.
Cr3R = Cross 3 right Slip next st onto cable
needle and leave at back of work, K2, then P (or
K depending on point in patt) st from cable
needle.
Cr3L = Cross 3 left Slip next 2 sts onto cable
needle and leave at front of work, P (or K
depending on point in patt) next st, then K2
from cable needle.

BACK

Cast on 70 (78: 84: 92: 98) sts using 3¼mm
(US 3) needles.
Row 1 (RS): P2 (1:0:0:1), K2 (2:1:0:2), (P3, K2)
5 (6:7:8:8) times, P2, K8, P2, (K2, P3) 5 (6:7:8:8)
times, K2 (2:1:0:2), P2 (1:0:0:1).
Row 2: K2 (1:0:0:1), P2 (2:1:0:2), (K3, P2)
5 (6:7:8:8) times, K2, P8, K2, (P2, K3) 5 (6:7:8:8)
times, P2 (2:1:0:2), K2 (1:0:0:1).
These 2 rows form rib.
Work in rib for a further 4 rows, ending with a
WS row.
Change to 4mm (US 6) needles.
Starting and ending rows as indicated and
repeating the 10 row repeat throughout, cont in
patt from chart for body until back measures
12 (16:19:22:26) cm, ending with a WS row.
Shape armholes
Keeping patt correct, cast off 6 sts at beg of next
2 rows. 58 (66:72:80:86) sts.
Cont straight until armhole measures 12 (13:14:
15:16) cm, ending with a WS row.
Shape shoulders and back neck
Cast off 4 (5:6:7:7) sts at beg of next 2 rows.
50 (56:60:66:72) sts.
Next row (RS): Cast off 4 (5:6:7:7) sts, patt
until there are 8 (9:9:10:12) sts on right needle
and turn, leaving rem sts on a holder.
Work each side of neck separately.
Cast off 4 sts at beg of next row.
Cast off rem 4 (5:5:6:8) sts.
With RS facing, rejoin yarn to rem sts, cast off
centre 26 (28:30:32:34) sts dec 4 sts across top
of central cable, patt to end.
Complete to match first side, reversing shapings.

FRONT

Work as given for back until 12 (12:14:14:14)
rows less have been worked than on back to

start of shoulder shaping, ending with a WS row.
Shape neck
Next row (RS): Patt 21 (24:27:30:32) sts and
turn, leaving rem sts on a holder.
Work each side of neck separately.
Dec 1 st at neck edge of next 9 rows, then on
foll 0 (0:1:1:1) alt row. 12 (15:17:20:22) sts.
Work 2 rows, ending with a WS row.
Shape shoulder
Cast off 4 (5:6:7:7) sts at beg of next and foll
alt row.
Work 1 row. Cast off rem 4 (5:5:6:8) sts.
With RS facing, slip centre 16 (18:18:20:22) sts
onto a holder, rejoin yarn to rem sts, patt to end.
Complete to match first side, reversing shapings.

LEFT SLEEVE

Cast on 40 (42:44:46:48) sts using 3¼mm
(US 3) needles.
Row 1 (RS): K0 (0:1:0:0), P2 (3:3:0:1), ★K2,
P3, rep from ★ to last 3 (4:0:1:2) sts, K2 (2:0:1:2),
P1 (2:0:0:0).
Row 2: K1 (2:0:0:0), P2 (2:0:1:2), ★K3, P2,
rep from ★ to last 2 (3:4:0:1) sts, K2 (3:3:0:1),
P0 (0:1:0:0).
These 2 rows form rib.
Work in rib for a further 4 rows, ending with a
WS row.
Change to 4mm (US 6) needles.
Starting and ending rows as indicated and
repeating the 10 row repeat throughout, cont
in patt from chart for left sleeve, shaping sides
by inc 1 st at each end of 3rd and every foll
4th (4th:4th:6th:6th) row to 48 (56:66:52:58) sts,
then on every foll alt (alt:alt:4th:4th) row until
there are 66 (70:74:78:82) sts.
Cont straight until sleeve measures 15 (18:22:
28:32) cm, ending with a WS row.
Cast off in patt.

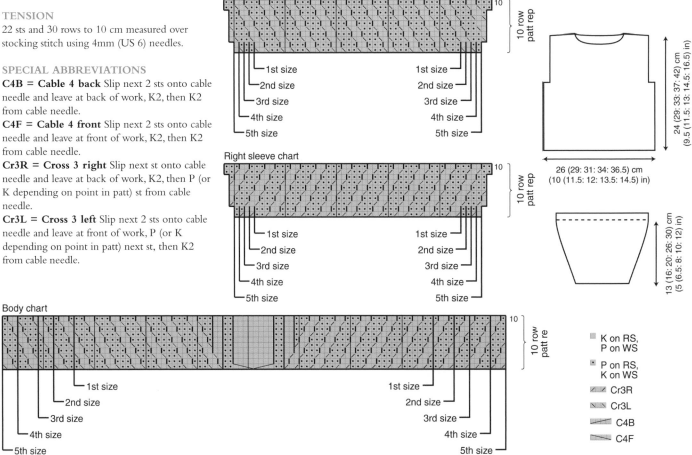

Left sleeve chart

10
10 row patt rep

1st size
2nd size
3rd size
4th size
5th size

1st size
2nd size
3rd size
4th size
5th size

Right sleeve chart

10
10 row patt rep

1st size
2nd size
3rd size
4th size
5th size

1st size
2nd size
3rd size
4th size
5th size

24 (29: 33: 37: 42) cm
(9.5 (11.5: 13: 14.5: 16.5) in)

26 (29: 31: 34: 36.5) cm
(10 (11.5: 12: 13.5: 14.5) in)

13 (16: 20: 26: 30) cm
(5 (6.5: 8: 10: 12) in)

Body chart

10
10 row patt re

1st size
2nd size
3rd size
4th size
5th size

1st size
2nd size
3rd size
4th size
5th size

K on RS, P on WS
P on RS, K on WS
Cr3R
Cr3L
C4B
C4F

Cast on 40 (42: 44: 46: 48) sts using 3¼mm (US 3) needles.
Row 1 (RS): P1 (2: 0: 0: 0), K2 (2: 0: 1: 2), ★P3, K2, rep from ★ to last 2 (3: 4: 0: 1) sts, P2 (3: 3: 0: 1), K0 (0: 1: 0: 0).
Row 2: P0 (0: 1: 0: 0), K2 (3: 3: 0: 1), ★P2, K3, rep from ★ to last 3 (4: 0: 1: 2) sts, P2 (2: 0: 1: 2), K1 (2: 0: 0: 0).
These 2 rows form rib.
Work in rib for a further 4 rows, ending with a WS row.
Change to 4mm (US 6) needles.

Complete to match left sleeve, foll chart for right sleeve.

PRESS as described on the information page. Join right shoulder seam using back stitch, or mattress st if preferred.
Neckband
With RS facing and using 3¼mm (US 3) needles, pick up and knit 13 (13: 15: 15: 15) sts down left side of neck, patt across 16 (18: 18: 20: 22) sts from front holder, pick up and knit 13 (13: 15: 15: 15) sts up right side of neck, then

30 (32: 32: 34: 36) sts from back.
72 (76: 80: 84: 88) sts.
Row 1 (WS): P1 (0: 0: 1: 0), K2 (2: 0: 2: 2), (P2, K2) 11 (12: 13: 13: 14) times, P8, (K2, P2) 4 (4: 5: 5: 5) times, K1 (2: 0: 1: 2).
Row 2: P1 (2: 0: 1: 2), (K2, P2) 4 (4: 5: 5: 5) times, patt 8 sts, (P2, K2) 11 (12: 13: 13: 14) times, P2 (2: 0: 2: 2), K1 (0: 0: 1: 0).
Rep last 2 rows until neckband measures 3 (3: 4: 4: 5) cm.
Cast off **loosely** in patt.
See information page for finishing instructions, setting in sleeves using the square set-in method.

Design number 13

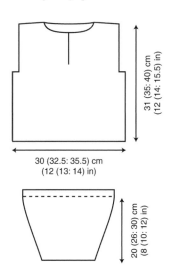

HANS

	3rd	4th	5th	size
To fit age	1-2	2-3	4-5	years
To fit chest	51	56	61	cm
	20	22	24	in
Rowan Wool Cotton				
A Misty 903	3	4	5	x 50gm
B Inky 908	1	2	2	x 50gm

1 pair 3¼mm (no 10) (US 3) needles
1 pair 4mm (no 8) (US 6) needles

22 sts and 30 rows to 10 cm measured over stocking stitch using 4mm (US 6) needles.

Cast on 66 (70: 78) sts using 3¼mm (US 3) needles and yarn A.
Row 1 (RS): K2, ★P2, K2, rep from ★ to end.
Row 2: P2, ★K2, P2, rep from ★ to end.
These 2 rows form rib.
Work in rib for a further 4 rows, inc 0 (1: 0) st at each end of last row and ending with a WS row. 66 (72: 78) sts.
Change to 4mm (US 6) needles.
Beg with a K row, work in st st for 4 rows.
Join in yarn B and cont in striped st st as folls:

Using yarn B, work 2 rows.
Using yarn A, work 6 rows.
Last 8 rows form striped st st.
Cont in striped st st until back measures 17 (20: 24) cm, ending with a WS row.
Shape armholes
Keeping stripes correct, cast off 6 sts at beg of next 2 rows. 54 (60: 66) sts.★★
Cont straight until armhole measures 14 (15: 16) cm, ending with a WS row.
Shape shoulders and back neck
Cast off 5 (6: 7) sts at beg of next 2 rows. 44 (48: 52) sts.
Next row (RS): Cast off 5 (6: 7) sts, K until there are 10 sts on right needle and turn, leaving rem sts on a holder.
Work each side of neck separately.
Cast off 4 sts at beg of next row.
Cast off rem 6 sts.
With RS facing, rejoin appropriate yarn to rem sts, cast off centre 14 (16: 18) sts, K to end.
Complete to match first side, reversing shapings.

Work as given for back until armhole measures 1.5 (2.5: 3.5) cm, ending with a WS row.
Divide for front opening
Next row (RS): K23 (26: 29) and turn, leaving rem sts on a holder.
Work each side of neck separately.
Cont straight until 9 rows less have been worked than on back to start of shoulder shaping, ending with a RS row.
Shape neck
Keeping stripes correct, cast off 1 (2: 3) sts at beg of next row. 22 (24: 26) sts.
Dec 1 st at neck edge of next 5 rows, then on foll alt row. 16 (18: 20) sts.
Work 1 row, ending with a WS row.
Shape shoulder
Cast off 5 (6: 7) sts at beg of next and foll alt row.
Work 1 row.
Cast off rem 6 sts.
With RS facing, rejoin appropriate yarn to rem sts, cast off centre 8 sts, K to end.
Complete to match first side, reversing shapings.

Cast on 34 (38: 38) sts using 3¼mm (US 3) needles and yarn A.
Work in rib as given for back for 6 rows, inc 1 (0: 1) st at each end of last row and ending with a WS row. 36 (38: 40) sts.
Change to 4mm (US 6) needles.
Beg with a K row and 4 rows using yarn A, cont in striped st st, inc 1 st at each end of 3rd and

every foll 4th row to 62 (52: 48) sts, then on every foll – (6th: 6th) row until there are – (66: 70) sts.
Cont straight until sleeve measures 22.5 (28.5: 32.5) cm, ending with a WS row.
Cast off.

PRESS as described on the information page. Join shoulder seams using back stitch, or mattress st if preferred.
Front bands (both alike)
With RS facing, using 3¼mm (US 3) needles and yarn A, pick up and knit 23 sts up one front opening edge between base of opening and neck shaping.
Row 1 (WS): K1, ★P1, K1, rep from ★ to end.
Row 2: K1, P1, ★yrn, P2tog, (K1, P1) twice, rep from ★ twice more, yrn, P2tog, K1.
Rows 3 and 4: As row 1.
Cast off in moss st (on WS).
Collar
Cast on 62 (66: 70) sts using 3¼mm (US 3) needles and yarn A.
Row 1 (RS): (K1, P1) twice, K2, ★P2, K2, rep from ★ to last 4 sts, (P1, K1) twice.
Row 2: (K1, P1) twice, P2, ★K2, P2, rep from ★ to last 4 sts, (P1, K1) twice.
Rep these 2 rows until collar measures 6 cm.
Cast off in patt.
See information page for finishing instructions, setting in sleeves using the square set-in method. Positioning ends of collar halfway across top of front bands, sew cast-on edge of collar to neck edge. Using yarn A, make a twisted cord approx 60 cm long and thread through eyelet holes of front bands as in photograph.

31 (35: 40) cm
(12 (14: 15.5) in)

30 (32.5: 35.5) cm
(12 (13: 14) in)

20 (26: 30) cm
(8 (10: 12) in)

Duel

YARN

	1st	2nd	3rd	4th	5th	size
	months		years			
To fit age	0-6	6-12	1-2	2-3	4-5	
To fit chest	41	46	51	56	61	cm
	16	18	20	22	24	in

Rowan All Seasons Cotton

3 4 4 5 6 x 50gm

(photographed in Cloud 163)

NEEDLES

1 pair 4mm (no 8) (US 6) needles
1 pair 5mm (no 6) (US 8) needles

BUTTONS – 5 x 75324

TENSION

17 sts and 24 rows to 10 cm measured over
stocking stitch using 5mm (US 8) needles.

BACK

Cast on 42 (46: 52: 56: 60) sts using 4mm (US 6)
needles.
Row 1 (RS): K0 (0: 1: 0: 1), P2 (0: 2: 1: 2), ★K2,
P2, rep from ★ to last 0 (2: 1: 3: 1) sts, K0 (2: 1: 2:
1), P0 (0: 0: 1: 0).
Row 2: P0 (0: 1: 0: 1), K2 (0: 2: 1: 2), ★P2, K2,
rep from ★ to last 0 (2: 1: 3: 1) sts, P0 (2: 1: 2: 1),
K0 (0: 0: 1: 0).
These 2 rows form rib.
Work in rib for a further 4 (4: 6: 6: 8) rows,
ending with a WS row.
Change to 5mm (US 8) needles.
Beg with a K row, work in st st for 2 rows,
ending with a WS row.
Next row (inc) (RS): K2, M1, K to last 2 sts,
M1, K2.
Working all side seam increases as set by last row,
inc 1 st at each end of every foll 4th (6th: 8th: 10th:
12th) row until there are 48 (52: 58: 62: 66) sts.
Work a further 3 (3: 5: 5: 7) rows, ending with a WS
row. (Back should measure 8 (10: 13: 15: 18) cm.)
Shape armholes
Cast off 5 sts at beg of next 2 rows.
38 (42: 48: 52: 56) sts.
Cont straight until armhole measures 13 (14: 15:
16: 17) cm, ending with a WS row.

Shape shoulders and back neck

Cast off 4 (4: 5: 6: 6) sts at beg of next 2 rows.
30 (34: 38: 40: 44) sts.
Next row (RS): Cast off 4 (4: 5: 6: 6) sts,
K until there are 8 (9: 10: 9: 11) sts on right
needle and turn, leaving rem sts on a holder.
Work each side of neck separately.
Cast off 4 sts at beg of next row.
Cast off rem 4 (5: 6: 5: 7) sts.
With RS facing, rejoin yarn to rem sts, cast off
centre 6 (8: 8: 10: 10) sts, K to end.
Complete to match first side, reversing shapings.

POCKET LININGS (make 2)

Cast on 10 (12: 14: 15: 16) sts using 5mm (US 8)
needles.
Beg with a K row, work in st st for 4 rows.
Break yarn and leave sts on a holder.

LEFT FRONT

Cast on 26 (28: 31: 33: 35) sts using 4mm (US 6)
needles.
Row 1 (RS): K0 (0: 1: 0: 1), P2 (0: 2: 1: 2), ★K2,
P2, rep from ★ to last 8 sts, K2, (P1, K1) 3 times.
Row 2: (K1, P1) twice, K2, ★P2, K2, rep from ★
to last 0 (2: 1: 3: 1) sts, P0 (2: 1: 2: 1), K0 (0: 0: 1: 0).
These 2 rows set the sts – front opening edge 5 sts
in moss st and all other sts in rib.
Cont as set for a further 0 (0: 2: 2: 4) rows,
ending with a WS row.
Next row (buttonhole row) (RS): Patt to last
3 sts, yrn, P2tog (to make a buttonhole), K1.
Work a further 2 rows, ending with a RS row.
Next row (WS): (K1, P1) 3 times and slip these
6 sts onto a holder, M1, rib to end.
21 (23: 26: 28: 30) sts.
Change to 5mm (US 8) needles.
Beg with a K row and working all side seam
increases 2 sts in from ends of rows as given for
back, work in st st for 4 rows, inc 1 st at beg of
3rd of these rows and ending with a WS row.
22 (24: 27: 29: 31) sts.
Divide for pocket
Next row (RS): K12 (12: 13: 14: 15), slip rem
10 (12: 14: 15: 16) sts onto a holder for pocket
front and, in their place, K across 10 (12: 14: 15:
16) sts of first pocket lining. 22 (24: 27: 29: 31) sts.
Work on this set of sts only for side front and
pocket lining.
Inc 1 st at beg of 2nd (4th: 6th: 8th: 10th) and
every foll 4th (6th: 8th: 10th: 12th) row until
there are 24 (26: 29: 31: 33) sts.
1st and 2nd sizes
Work 3 rows, ending with a WS row.
Shape armhole
Cast off 5 sts at beg of next row. 19 (21: –: –: –) sts.
Work a further 4 (0: –: –: –) rows, ending with a
RS row.
All sizes
Break yarn and leave sts on a holder.
Shape pocket front
With RS facing, rejoin yarn to 10 (12: 14: 15:
16) sts from holder for pocket front and work
17 (17: 17: 19: 23) rows, ending with a RS row.
Join sections
Next row (WS): Holding RS of pocket lining
against WS of pocket front, P tog first st of
pocket lining with first st of pocket front, P tog
rem 9 (11: 13: 14: 15) sts of pocket front with
next 9 (11: 13: 14: 15) sts of pocket lining, then
P rem 9 (9: 15: 16: 17) sts of side front.
19 (21: 29: 31: 33) sts.
3rd, 4th and 5th sizes
Work a further – (–: 4: 4: 6) rows, ending with a
WS row.

Shape armhole

Cast off 5 sts at beg of next row. – (–: 24: 26: 28) sts.
All sizes
Cont straight until 7 (7: 9: 9: 9) rows less have
been worked than on back to start of shoulder
shaping, ending with a RS row.
Shape neck
Cast off 4 (5: 4: 5: 5) sts at beg of next row.
15 (16: 20: 21: 23) sts.
Dec 1 st at neck edge of next 3 rows, then on
foll 0 (0: 1: 1: 1) alt row. 12 (13: 16: 17: 19) sts.
Work 3 rows, ending with a WS row.
Shape shoulder
Cast off 4 (4: 5: 6: 6) sts at beg of next and foll
alt row.
Work 1 row. Cast off rem 4 (5: 6: 5: 7) sts.

RIGHT FRONT

Cast on 26 (28: 31: 33: 35) sts using 4mm (US 6)
needles.
Row 1 (RS): (K1, P1) 3 times, ★K2, P2, rep
from ★ to last 0 (2: 1: 3: 1) sts, K0 (2: 1: 2: 1),
P0 (0: 0: 1: 0).
Row 2: P0 (0: 1: 0: 1), K2 (0: 2: 1: 2), ★P2, K2,
rep from ★ to last 4 sts, (P1, K1) twice.
These 2 rows set the sts – front opening edge 5 sts
in moss st and all other sts in rib.
Cont as set for a further 3 (3: 5: 5: 7) rows,
ending with a RS row.
Next row (WS): Rib to last 6 sts, M1 and turn,
leaving last 6 sts on a holder. 21 (23: 26: 28: 30) sts.
Change to 5mm (US 8) needles.
Beg with a K row and working all side seam
increases as given for back, work in st st for 4
rows, inc 1 st at end of 3rd of these rows and
ending with a WS row. 22 (24: 27: 29: 31) sts.
Divide for pocket
Next row (RS): K10 (12: 14: 15: 16) and turn,
leaving rem 12 (12: 13: 14: 15) sts on a holder
for side front.
Work on this set of sts only for pocket front.
Work a further 16 (16: 16: 18: 22) rows, ending
with a RS row.
Break yarn and leave sts on a holder.
Shape side front and pocket lining
With RS facing, K across 10 (12: 14: 15: 16) sts
of second lining, then K across 12 (12: 13: 14:
15) sts left on first holder. 22 (24: 27: 29: 31) sts.
Inc 1 st at end of 2nd (4th: 6th: 8th: 10th) and
every foll 4th (6th: 8th: 10th: 12th) row until
there are 24 (26: 29: 31: 33) sts.
1st and 2nd sizes
Work 4 rows, ending with a RS row.

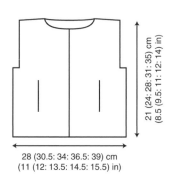

28 (30.5: 34: 36.5: 39) cm
(11 (12: 13.5: 14.5: 15.5) in)

21 (24: 28: 31: 35) cm
(8.5 (9.5: 11: 12: 14) in)

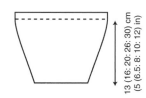

13 (16: 20: 26: 30) cm
(5 (6.5: 8: 10: 12) in)

1st size

Shape armhole

Cast off 5 sts at beg of next row. 19 (-: -: -: -) sts.
Work a further 3 (-: -: -: -: -) rows, ending with a RS row.

All sizes

Join sections

Next row (WS): Cast off 0 (5: 0: 0: 0) sts, P until there are 9 (9: 15: 16: 17) sts on right needle, holding RS of pocket lining against WS of pocket front, P tog next st of pocket front with first st of pocket lining, P tog rem 9 (11: 13: 14: 15) sts of pocket front with rem 9 (11: 13: 14: 15) sts of pocket lining. 19 (21: 29: 31: 33) sts.
Complete to match left front, reversing shapings.

SLEEVES (both alike)

Cast on 26 (30: 30: 34: 34) sts using 4mm (US 6) needles.
Row 1 (RS): K2, *P2, K2, rep from * to end.
Row 2: P2, *K2, P2, rep from * to end.
These 2 rows form rib.
Work in rib for a further 4 (4: 6: 6: 8) rows, inc 1 (0: 1: 0: 1) st at each end of last row and ending with a WS row. 28 (30: 32: 34: 36) sts.
Change to 5mm (US 8) needles.
Beg with a K row and working all increases as

given for back, cont in st st, shaping sides by inc 1 st at each end of 3rd (3rd: 3rd: 5th: 5th) and every foll 4th (4th: 4th: 6th: 6th) row to 34 (42: 46: 42: 44) sts, then on every foll alt (alt: alt: 4th: 4th) row until there are 42 (46: 50: 54: 58) sts.
Cont straight until sleeve measures 16 (19: 23: 29: 33) cm, ending with a WS row. Cast off.

MAKING UP

PRESS as described on the information page. Join shoulder seams using back stitch, or mattress st if preferred.

Button band

Slip 6 sts left on right front holder onto 4mm (US 6) needles and rejoin yarn with WS facing.
Cont in moss st as set until band, when slightly stretched, fits up right front opening edge to neck shaping. Cast off.
Slip stitch band in place.
Mark positions for 5 buttons on this band – first to come level with buttonhole already worked in left front, last to come 1.5 cm below neck shaping and rem 3 buttons evenly spaced between.

Buttonhole band

Slip 6 sts left on left front holder onto 4mm (US 6) needles and rejoin yarn with RS facing.
Cont in moss st as set until band, when slightly

stretched, fits up right front opening edge to neck shaping with the addition of a further 4 buttonholes worked to correspond with positions marked for buttons as folls:
Buttonhole row (RS): P1, K1, P1, yrn, P2tog (to make a buttonhole), K1.
When band is complete, cast off.
Slip stitch band in place.

Collar

Cast on 48 (52: 60: 64: 68) sts using 4mm (US 6) needles.
Row 1 (RS): K1, (P1, K1) twice, P2, *K2, P2, rep from * to last 5 sts, (K1, P1) twice, K1.
Row 2: K1, (P1, K1) twice, K2, *P2, K2, rep from * to last 5 sts, (K1, P1) twice, K1.
Rep these 2 rows until collar measures 6.5 (6.5: 7.5: 7.5: 8.5) cm. Cast off in patt.

Pocket borders (both alike)

With RS facing and using 4mm (US 6) needles, pick up and knit 14 (14: 14: 18: 18) sts along pocket opening edge.
Beg with row 2, work in rib as given for sleeves for 3 rows. Cast off in rib.
See information page for finishing instructions, setting in sleeves using the square set-in method. Positioning ends of collar halfway across top of bands, sew cast-on edge of collar to neck edge.

DESIGN NUMBER 15

SNUG

YARN

Rowan 4 ply Soft

	s	m	l	
Two colour hat				
A Black 383	1	1	1	x 50gm
B Smokey Joe 384	1	1	1	x 50gm
One colour hat	1	2	2	x 50gm
(photographed in Puff 385)				

NEEDLES

1 pair 3mm (no 11) (US 2/3) needles
1 pair 3¼mm (no 10) (US 3) needles

TENSION

28 sts and 36 rows to 10 cm measured over stocking stitch using 3¼mm (US 3) needles.

MEASUREMENTS

Finished hat measures approx 38 (41: 44) cm, 15 (16: 17½) in, around head.

TWO COLOUR HAT

Cast on 107 (115: 123) sts using 3mm (US 2/3) needles and yarn A.
Beg with a K row, work in st st for 8 rows.
Change to 3¼mm (US 3) needles.
Cont straight until hat measures 17 (18: 19) cm, ending with a WS row.
Break off yarn A and join in yarn B.
Cont straight until hat measures 24 (25: 26) cm, ending with a WS row.

Shape top

Large size only
Row 1 (RS): K1, K2tog, *K27, K3tog tbl, rep from * twice more, K27, K2tog tbl, K1.
115 sts.
Work 1 row.

Medium and large size only
Next row (RS): K1, K2tog, *K25, K3tog tbl, rep from * twice more, K25, K2tog tbl, K1. 107 sts.
Work 1 row.

All sizes
Next row (RS): K1, K2tog, *K23, K3tog tbl, rep from * twice more, K23, K2tog tbl, K1. 99 sts.
Work 1 row.
Next row: K1, K2tog, *K21, K3tog tbl, rep from * twice more, K21, K2tog tbl, K1. 91 sts.
Work 1 row.
Next row: K1, K2tog, *K19, K3tog tbl, rep from * twice more, K19, K2tog tbl, K1. 83 sts.
Work 1 row.
Next row: K1, K2tog, *K17, K3tog tbl, rep from * twice more, K17, K2tog tbl, K1. 75 sts.
Work 1 row.
Next row: K1, K2tog, *K15, K3tog tbl, rep from * twice more, K15, K2tog tbl, K1. 67 sts.
Work 1 row.
Next row: K1, K2tog, *K13, K3tog tbl, rep from * twice more, K13, K2tog tbl, K1. 59 sts.
Work 1 row.
Next row: K1, K2tog, *K11, K3tog tbl, rep

from * twice more, K11, K2tog tbl, K1. 51 sts.
Next row: P1, P2tog tbl, *P9, P3tog tbl, rep from * twice more, P9, P2tog, P1. 43 sts.
Next row: K1, K2tog, *K7, K3tog tbl, rep from * twice more, K7, K2tog tbl, K1. 35 sts.

Next row: P1, P2tog tbl, *P5, P3tog tbl, rep from * twice more, P5, P2tog, P1. 27 sts.
Next row: K1, K2tog, *K3, K3tog tbl, rep from * twice more, K3, K2tog tbl, K1. 19 sts.
Next row: P1, P2tog tbl, *P1, P3tog tbl, rep from * twice more, P1, P2tog, P1. 11 sts.
Break yarn and thread through rem 11 sts.
Pull up tight and fasten off securely.
Join back seam.
Fold 8 cm to inside around cast-on edge and slip stitch in place.

ONE COLOUR HAT

Work as for two colour hat but using same colour throughout.

STRAWBERRY BUD

YARN

	1st	2nd	3rd	4th	5th size
	months		years		
To fit age	0-6	6-12	1-2	2-3	4-5
To fit chest	41	46	51	56	61 cm
	16	18	20	22	24 in

Rowan 4 ply Cotton

A Orchid	120	2	2	3	3	4 x 50gm
B Fresh	131	1	1	1	1	1 x 50gm
C Fandango	128	1	1	1	1	1 x 50gm

NEEDLES

1 pair 2¼mm (no 13) (US 1) needles
1 pair 3mm (no 11) (US 2/3) needles

BUTTONS – 7 x 75320

TENSION

28 sts and 38 rows to 10 cm measured over
stocking stitch using 3mm (US 2/3) needles.

SPECIAL ABBREVIATION

MB = Make bobble using yarn C as folls: K into
front, back, front, back and front again of next st,
turn, P5, turn, slip 2 sts, K3tog, pass 2 slipped sts
over.

BACK

Cast on 59 (67: 75: 83: 91) sts using 2¼mm
(US 1) needles and yarn A.
Row 1 (RS): K1, ★P1, K1, rep from ★ to end.
Row 2: As row 1.
These 2 rows form moss st.
Work in moss st for a further 5 rows, ending
with a RS row.
Change to 3mm (US 2/3) needles.
Purl 1 row.
Using the **intarsia** technique as described on
the information page, starting and ending rows
as indicated and repeating the 24 row repeat
throughout, cont in patt from chart, which is
worked entirely in st st beg with a K row, as
folls:
Cont straight until back measures 8 (10: 13: 16:
20) cm, ending with a WS row.
Shape armholes
Keeping patt correct, cast off 6 sts at beg of next
2 rows. 47 (55: 63: 71: 79) sts.
Cont straight until armhole measures 11 (12: 13:
14: 15) cm, ending with a WS row.
Shape shoulders and back neck
Cast off 4 (5: 6: 7: 8) sts at beg of next 2 rows.
39 (45: 51: 57: 63) sts.
Next row (RS): Cast off 4 (5: 6: 7: 8) sts, patt
until there are 8 (9: 10: 11: 12) sts on right
needle and turn, leaving rem sts on a holder.
Work each side of neck separately.
Cast off 4 sts at beg of next row.
Cast off rem 4 (5: 6: 7: 8) sts.
With RS facing, rejoin yarns to rem sts, cast off
centre 15 (17: 19: 21: 23) sts, patt to end.
Complete to match first side, reversing shapings.

LEFT FRONT

Cast on 35 (39: 43: 47: 51) sts using 2¼mm
(US 1) needles and yarn A.
Work in moss st as given for back for 6 rows,
ending with a WS row.
Row 7 (RS): Moss st to last 6 sts, M1 and turn,

leaving last 6 sts on a holder. 30 (34: 38: 42: 46) sts.
Change to 3mm (US 2/3) needles.
Purl 1 row.
Starting and ending rows as indicated, cont in
patt from chart as folls:
Cont straight until left front matches back to
beg of armhole shaping, ending with a WS row.
Shape armhole
Keeping patt correct, cast off 6 sts at beg of next
row. 24 (28: 32: 36: 40) sts.
Cont straight until 11 (11: 13: 13: 13) rows less
have been worked than on back to start of
shoulder shaping, ending with a RS row.
Shape neck
Cast off 6 (7: 7: 8: 9) sts at beg of next row.
18 (21: 25: 28: 31) sts.
Dec 1 st at neck edge of next 5 rows, then on
foll 1 (1: 2: 2: 2) alt rows. 12 (15: 18: 21: 24) sts.
Work 3 rows, ending with a WS row.
Shape shoulder
Cast off 4 (5: 6: 7: 8) sts at beg of next and foll
alt row.
Work 1 row.
Cast off rem 4 (5: 6: 7: 8) sts.

RIGHT FRONT

Cast on 35 (39: 43: 47: 51) sts using 2¼mm
(US 1) needles and yarn A.
Work in moss st as given for back for 4 rows,
ending with a WS row.
Row 5 (buttonhole row) (RS): Moss st 1 st,
work 2 tog, yrn (to make a buttonhole), moss st
to end.
Work in moss st for 1 row more, ending with a
WS row.
Row 7 (RS): Moss st 6 sts and slip these sts
onto a holder, M1, moss st to end.
30 (34: 38: 42: 46) sts.
Change to 3mm (US 2/3) needles and complete
to match left front, reversing shapings.

SLEEVES (both alike)

Cast on 41 (43: 45: 47: 49) sts using 2¼mm
(US 1) needles and yarn A.
Work in moss st as given for back for 7 rows,
ending with a RS row.
Change to 3mm (US 2/3) needles.
Purl 1 row.

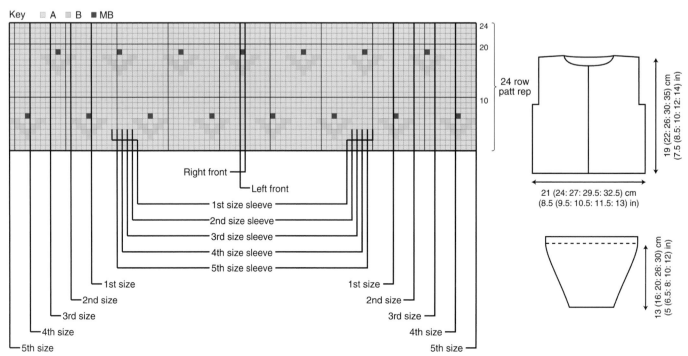

Key ☐ A ▨ B ■ MB

24 row patt rep

Right front
Left front
1st size sleeve
2nd size sleeve
3rd size sleeve
4th size sleeve
5th size sleeve

1st size
2nd size
3rd size
4th size
5th size

1st size
2nd size
3rd size
4th size
5th size

19 (22: 26: 30: 35) cm
(7.5 (8.5: 10: 12: 14) in)

21 (24: 27: 29.5: 32.5) cm
(8.5 (9.5: 10.5: 11.5: 13) in)

13 (16: 20: 26: 30) cm
(5 (6.5: 8: 10: 12) in)

Starting and ending rows as indicated, cont in patt from chart, shaping sides by inc 1 st at each end of 3rd and every foll 4th (4th: 6th: 6th: 6th) row to 55 (65: 55: 69: 79) sts, then on every foll alt (alt: 4th: 4th: 4th) row until there are 61 (67: 73: 79: 85) sts, taking inc sts into patt.
Cont straight until sleeve measures 15 (18: 22: 28: 32) cm, ending with a WS row. Cast off.

MAKING UP

PRESS as described on the information page. Join both shoulder seams using back stitch, or mattress st if preferred.

Button band
Slip 6 sts from left front holder onto 2¼mm (US 1) needles and rejoin yarn A with RS facing.
Cont in moss st as set until band, when slightly stretched, fits up left front opening edge to neck shaping, ending with a WS row.
Break yarn. Slip st band in place.
Mark positions for 7 buttons on this band – first to come level with buttonhole already worked in right front, last to come just above neck shaping and rem 5 buttons evenly spaced between.

Buttonhole band
Slip 6 sts from right front holder onto 2¼mm (US 1) needles and rejoin yarn A with WS facing.
Cont in moss st as set until band, when slightly stretched, fits up right front opening edge to neck shaping, ending with a WS row and with the addition of a further 5 buttonholes worked to correspond with positions marked for buttons as folls:
Buttonhole row (RS): Moss st 1 st, work 2 tog, yrn (to make a buttonhole), moss st 3 sts.

When band is complete, do NOT break yarn. Slip st band in place.

Neckband
With RS facing, using 2¼mm (US 1) needles and yarn A, moss st 6 sts of buttonhole band, pick up and knit 19 (20: 23: 24: 25) sts up right side of neck, 23 (25: 27: 29: 31) sts from back, and 19 (20: 23: 24: 25) sts down left side of neck, then moss st 6 sts of button band.
73 (77: 85: 89: 93) sts.
Work in moss st as set by bands for 3 rows, ending with a WS row.
Row 4 (RS): Moss st 1 st, work 2 tog, yrn (to make 7th buttonhole), moss st to end.
Work in moss st for a further 2 rows.
Cast off in moss st (on WS).
See information page for finishing instructions, setting in sleeves using the square set-in method.

DESIGN NUMBER 17

ARCHIE

YARN

	1st	2nd	3rd	4th	5th	size
	months		years			
To fit age	0-6	6-12	1-2	2-3	4-5	
To fit chest	41	46	51	56	61	cm
	16	18	20	22	24	in
Rowan 4 ply Soft						
	3	4	5	6	7 x 50gm	

(photographed in Smoky Joe 384)

NEEDLES

1 pair 2¾mm (no 12) (US 2) needles
1 pair 3¼mm (no 10) (US 3) needles

BUTTONS – 5 x 75315

TENSION

28 sts and 36 rows to 10 cm measured over stocking stitch using 3¼mm (US 3) needles.

BACK

Cast on 70 (78: 86: 94: 102) sts using 2¾mm (US 2) needles.
Beg with a K row, work in st st for 8 rows, ending with a WS row.
Change to 3¼mm (US 3) needles.
Cont in st st until back measures 15 (18: 21: 24: 28) cm, ending with a WS row.
Shape armholes
Cast off 6 sts at beg of next 2 rows.
58 (66: 74: 82: 90) sts.
Cont straight until armhole measures 12 (13: 14: 15: 16) cm, ending with a WS row.
Shape shoulders and back neck
Cast off 6 (7: 8: 9: 10) sts at beg of next 2 rows.
46 (52: 58: 64: 70) sts.
Next row (RS): Cast off 6 (7: 8: 9: 10) sts, K until there are 9 (10: 11: 12: 13) sts on right needle and turn, leaving rem sts on a holder.
Work each side of neck separately.
Cast off 4 sts at beg of next row.
Cast off rem 5 (6: 7: 8: 9) sts.
With RS facing, rejoin yarns to rem sts, cast off centre 16 (18: 20: 22: 24) sts, K to end.
Complete to match first side, reversing shapings.

POCKET LININGS (make 2)

Cast on 19 (20: 21: 22: 23) sts using 3¼mm (US 3) needles.
Beg with a K row, work in st st for 21 (23: 25: 27: 29) rows, ending with a RS row.
Break yarn and leave sts on a holder.

RIGHT FRONT

Cast on 32 (36: 40: 44: 48) sts using 2¾mm (US 2) needles.
Beg with a K row, work in st st for 1 row.
Inc 1 st at end of next row and at same edge of next 6 rows, ending with a WS row.
39 (43: 47: 51: 55) sts.
Change to 3¼mm (US 3) needles.
Cont in st st, inc 1 st at shaped edge of next 2 rows.
41 (45: 49: 53: 57) sts.
Next row (RS): Inc in first st, K1, sl 1 purlwise (this st forms front opening edge fold line), K to end.
Next row: P to last st, inc in last st.
Next row: Inc in first st, K3, sl 1 purlwise, K to end.
Next row: P to last st, inc in last st.
45 (49: 53: 57: 61) sts.
Next row (RS): K6, sl 1 purlwise, K to end.
Next row: Purl.
These 2 rows set the sts.
Cont as set for a further 14 (16: 18: 20: 22) rows, ending with a WS row.
Place pocket
Next row (RS): Patt 19 (21: 23: 25: 27) sts,
cast off next 19 (20: 21: 22: 23) sts, K to end.
Next row: P7 (8: 9: 10: 11), P across 19 (20: 21: 22: 23) sts of first pocket lining, P to end.
Cont as set until right front matches back to beg of armhole shaping, ending with a RS row.
Shape armhole
Cast off 6 sts at beg of next row.
39 (43: 47: 51: 55) sts.
Cont straight until 12 (12: 14: 14: 14) rows less have been worked than on back to start of shoulder shaping, ending with a **WS** row.
Shape neck
Cast off 15 (16: 16: 17: 18) sts at beg of next row.
24 (27: 31: 34: 37) sts.
Dec 1 st at neck edge of next 6 rows, then on foll 1 (1: 2: 2: 2) alt rows. 17 (20: 23: 26: 29) sts.
Work 4 rows, ending with a **RS** row.
Shape shoulder
Cast off 6 (7: 8: 9: 10) sts at beg of next and foll alt row.
Work 1 row. Cast off rem 5 (6: 7: 8: 9) sts.
Mark positions for 5 buttons on this front – first to come 4 rows below pocket opening, last to come 1.2 cm below neck shaping, and rem 3 buttons evenly spaced between.

LEFT FRONT

Cast on 32 (36: 40: 44: 48) sts using 2¾mm (US 2) needles.
Beg with a K row, work in st st for 1 row.
Inc 1 st at beg of next row and at same edge of next 6 rows, ending with a WS row.
39 (43: 47: 51: 55) sts.
Change to 3¼mm (US 3) needles.
Cont in st st, inc 1 st at shaped edge of next 2 rows.
41 (45: 49: 53: 57) sts.
Next row (RS): K to last 3 sts, sl 1 purlwise (this st forms front opening edge fold line), K1, inc in last st.
Next row: Inc in first st, P to end.
Next row: K to last 5 sts, sl 1 purlwise, K3, inc in last st.
Next row: Inc in first st, P to end.
45 (49: 53: 57: 61) sts.
Next row (RS): K to last 7 sts, sl 1 purlwise, K6.
Next row: Purl.
These 2 rows set the sts.
Cont as set for a further 10 (12: 14: 16: 18) rows, ending with a WS row.
Next row (buttonhole row) (RS): K to last 10 sts, yfwd (to make a buttonhole), K2tog tbl, K1, sl 1 purlwise, K1, K2tog, yfwd (to make a buttonhole), K3.

Work 3 rows, ending with a WS row.

Place pocket

Next row (RS): K7 (8: 9: 10: 11), cast off next 19 (20: 21: 22: 23) sts, patt to end.

Next row: P19 (21: 23: 25: 27) sts, P across 19 (20: 21: 22: 23) sts of second pocket lining, P to end.

Complete to match right front, working a further 4 pairs of buttonholes as before to correspond with positions marked for buttons, and reversing shapings.

SLEEVES (both alike)

Cast on 41 (43: 45: 47: 49) sts using 2¾mm (US 2) needles.

Beg with a K row, work in st st for 8 rows, ending with a WS row.

Change to 3¼mm (US 3) needles.

Cont in st st for a further 8 rows, ending with a WS row.

Change to 3¼mm (US 3) needles.

Cont in st st, shaping sides by inc 1 st at each end of next and every foll alt (4th: 4th: 4th: 4th) row to 47 (73: 77: 69: 69) sts, then on every foll 4th (-: 6th: 6th: 6th) row until there are 67 (-: 79: 85: 91) sts.

Cont straight until sleeve measures 20 (23: 27: 33: 37) cm, ending with a WS row.

Cast off.

MAKING UP

PRESS as described on the information page.

Join both shoulder seams using back stitch, or mattress st if preferred.

Collar

Cast on 64 (68: 76: 80: 84) sts using 2¾mm (US 2) needles.

Beg with a K row, work in st st for 12 (12: 12: 14: 14) cm, ending with a WS row.

Cast off.

See information page for finishing instructions. Fold first 8 rows to inside around lower edge of body and sleeves and slip stitch in place. Fold front opening edges to inside along slip st fold line and slip stitch in place. Fold collar in half, RS facing, and sew across ends. Turn collar RS out. Placing ends of collar 3 sts in from front opening edges, sew cast-on and cast-off edge of collar to neck edge.

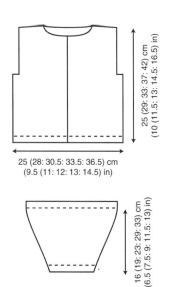

25 (29: 33: 37: 42) cm
(10 (11.5: 13: 14.5: 16.5) in)

25 (28: 30.5: 33.5: 36.5) cm
(9.5 (11: 12: 13: 14.5) in)

16 (19: 23: 29: 33) cm
(6.5 (7.5: 9: 11.5: 13) in)

HUSKY

YARN

	3rd	4th	5th	size
To fit age	1-2	2-3	4-5	years
To fit chest	51	56	61	cm
	20	22	24	in

Rowan Big Wool

| | 3 | 3 | 4 | x 100gm |

(photographed in Sugar Spun 016)

NEEDLES

1 pair 12mm (US 17) needles

TENSION

8 sts and 12 rows to 10 cm measured over stocking stitch using 12mm (US 17) needles.

BACK

Cast on 28 (30: 32) sts using 12mm (US 17) needles.

Row 1 (RS): P1 (0: 1), K2, *P2, K2, rep from * to last 1 (0: 1) st, P1 (0: 1).

Row 2: K1 (0: 1), P2, *K2, P2, rep from * to last 1 (0: 1) st, K1 (0: 1).

These 2 rows form rib.

Cont in rib for a further 4 rows, ending with a WS row.

Beg with a K row, cont in st st until back measures 15 (18: 22) cm, ending with a WS row.

Shape armholes

Cast off 3 sts at beg of next 2 rows. 22 (24: 26) sts.

Cont straight until armhole measures 17 (18: 19) cm, ending with a WS row.

Shape shoulders and back neck

Next row (RS): Cast off 3 sts, K until there are 6 (6: 7) sts on right needle and turn, leaving rem sts on a holder.

Work each side of neck separately.

Cast off 3 sts at beg of next row.

Cast off rem 3 (3: 4) sts.

With RS facing, rejoin yarn to rem sts, cast off centre 4 (6: 6) sts, K to end.

Complete to match first side, reversing shapings.

FRONT

Work as given for back until 6 rows less have been worked than on back to start of shoulder shaping, ending with a WS row.

Shape neck

Next row (RS): K9 (9: 10) and turn, leaving rem sts on a holder.

Work each side of neck separately.

Dec 1 st at neck edge of next 3 rows. 6 (6: 7) sts.

Work 2 rows, ending with a WS row.

Shape shoulder

Cast off 3 sts at beg of next row.

Work 1 row.

Cast off rem 3 (3: 4) sts.

With RS facing, slip centre 4 (6: 6) sts onto a holder, rejoin yarn to rem sts, K to end.

Complete to match first side, reversing shapings.

SLEEVES (both alike)

Cast on 14 (18: 18) sts using 12mm (US 17) needles.

Row 1 (RS): K2, *P2, K2, rep from * to end.

Row 2: P2, *K2, P2, rep from * to end.

These 2 rows form rib.

Cont in rib for a further 2 rows, ending with a WS row.

Beg with a K row, cont in st st, shaping sides by inc 1 st at each end of next and every foll alt (4th: 4th) row to 24 (28: 30) sts, then on every foll 4th (-: -) row until there are 26 (-: -) sts.

Cont straight until sleeve measures 19.5 (23.5: 27.5) cm, ending with a WS row.

Cast off **loosely**.

MAKING UP

PRESS as described on the information page.

Join right shoulder seam using back stitch, or mattress st if preferred.

Neckband

With RS facing and using 12mm (US 17) needles, pick up and knit 7 sts down left side of neck, knit across 4 (6: 6) sts from front holder, pick up and knit 7 sts up right side of neck, then 10 (12: 12) sts from back. 28 (32: 32) sts.

Row 1 (WS): *K2, P2, rep from * to end.

Rep this row twice more.

Cast off **loosely** in rib.

See information page for finishing instructions, setting in sleeves using the square set-in method.

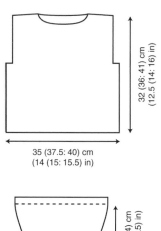

32 (36: 41) cm
(12.5 (14: 16) in)

35 (37.5: 40) cm
(14 (15: 15.5) in)

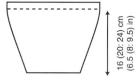

16 (20: 24) cm
(6.5 (8: 9.5) in)

HALLOW

YARN

	1st	2nd	3rd	4th	5th	size	
	months		years				
To fit age	0-6	6-12	1-2	2-3	4-5		
To fit chest	41	46	51	56	61	cm	
	16	18	20	22	24	in	

Rowan All Seasons Cotton

A Jazz	185	1	1	1	1	1	x	50gm
B Dp Marine	176	1	1	1	1	2	x	50gm
C Limedrop	197	1	1	1	1	2	x	50gm
D SeaView	166	1	1	2	2	2	x	50gm
E True Blue	165	1	1	1	1	1	x	50gm
F Purr	167	1	2	2	2	3	x	50gm
G Valour	181	1	1	2	2	2	x	50gm
H Kiss	175	1	1	1	1	1	x	50gm
J Jaunty	183	1	2	2	2	2	x	50gm

NEEDLES

1 pair 4mm (no 8) (US 6) needles
1 pair 5mm (no 6) (US 8) needles

TENSION

17 sts and 24 rows to 10 cm measured over stocking stitch using 5mm (US 8) needles.

STRIPE SEQUENCE

Beg with a K row, work in st st as folls:
Rows 1 and 2: Using yarn G.
Rows 3 and 4: Using yarn H.
Rows 5 and 6: Using yarn J.
Rows 7 and 8: Using yarn B.
Rows 9 and 10: Using yarn A.
Rows 11 and 12: Using yarn C.
Rows 13 and 14: Using yarn E.
Rows 15 and 16: Using yarn D.
Rows 17 and 18: Using yarn A.
Rows 19 and 20: Using yarn F.
Rows 21 and 22: Using yarn H.
Rows 23 and 24: Using yarn E.
Rows 25 and 26: Using yarn B.
Rows 27 and 28: Using yarn C.
Rows 29 and 30: Using yarn J.
Rows 31 and 32: Using yarn G.
Rows 33 and 34: Using yarn F.
Rows 35 and 36: Using yarn H.
Rows 37 and 38: Using yarn F.
Rows 39 and 40: Using yarn D.

Rows 41 and 42: Using yarn E.
Rows 43 and 44: Using yarn B.
Rows 45 and 46: Using yarn A.
Rows 47 and 48: Using yarn C.
Rows 49 and 50: Using yarn F.
Rows 51 and 52: Using yarn G.
Rows 53 and 54: Using yarn H.
Rows 55 and 56: Using yarn J.
Rows 57 and 58: Using yarn E.
Rows 59 and 60: Using yarn D.
These 60 rows form stripe sequence.

BACK

Cast on 43 (47: 53: 57: 61) sts using 4mm (US 6) needles and yarn F.
Beg with a K row, work in st st for 6 rows, ending with a WS row.
Change to 5mm (US 8) needles.
Beg with a K row and row 1, cont in st st in stripe sequence as detailed above until back measures 13 (16: 20: 24: 28) cm allowing first few rows to roll to RS, ending with a WS row.
Shape raglan armholes
Keeping stripes correct, cast off 3 sts at beg of next 2 rows. 37 (41: 47: 51: 55) sts.
1st size only
Work 4 rows, dec 1 st at each end of first of these rows. 35 sts.
All sizes
Dec 1 st at each end of next 1 (1: 3: 5: 5) rows, then on every foll alt row until 15 (15: 17: 17: 19) sts rem, then on foll row, ending with a WS row.
Cast off rem 13 (13: 15: 15: 17) sts.

LEFT FRONT

Cast on 23 (25: 28: 30: 32) sts using 4mm (US 6) needles and yarn F.
Beg with a K row, work in st st for 6 rows, ending with a WS row.
Change to 5mm (US 8) needles.
Beg with a K row and row 1, cont in st st in stripe sequence as detailed above until left front matches back to beg of raglan armhole shaping, ending with a WS row.
Shape raglan armhole
Keeping stripes correct, cast off 3 sts at beg of next row. 20 (22: 25: 27: 29) sts.
Work 1 row.
1st size only
Work 4 rows, dec 1 st at raglan armhole edge of first of these rows. 19 sts.
All sizes
Dec 1 st at raglan armhole edge of next 1 (1: 3: 5: 5) rows, then on every foll alt row until 14 (14: 16: 16: 17) sts rem, ending with a RS row.
Shape neck
Keeping stripes correct, cast off 7 (7: 7: 7: 8) sts at beg of next row. 7 (7: 9: 9: 9) sts.
Dec 1 st at neck edge of next 3 rows, then on foll 0 (0: 1: 1: 1) alt row **and at same time** dec 1 st at raglan armhole edge of next and every foll alt row. 2 sts.
Work 1 row.
Next row (RS): K2tog and fasten off.

RIGHT FRONT

Work to match left front, reversing shapings.

SLEEVES

Cast on 23 (25: 27: 29: 31) sts using 4mm (US 6) needles and yarn F.
Beg with a K row, work in st st for 6 rows, ending with a WS row.
Change to 5mm (US 8) needles.
Beg with a K row and row 1, cont in st st in

stripe sequence as detailed above, shaping sides by inc 1 st at each end of 3rd and every foll alt (4th: 4th: 6th: 8th) row to 33 (39: 35: 39: 43) sts, then on every foll 4th (-: 6th: 8th: 10th) row until there are 37 (-: 41: 43: 45) sts.
Cont straight until sleeve measures 13 (16: 20: 24: 28) cm allowing first few rows to roll to RS, ending with same stripe row as on back to beg of raglan shaping and a WS row.
Shape raglan
Keeping stripes correct, cast off 3 sts at beg of next 2 rows. 31 (33: 35: 37: 39) sts.
Dec 1 st at each end of next and every foll alt row until 13 sts rem.
Work 1 row, ending with a WS row.
Left sleeve only
Dec 1 st at each end of next row. 11 sts.
Cast off 2 sts at beg of next row, then dec 1 st at beg of foll row. 8 sts.
Rep last 2 rows once more. 5 sts.
Cast off 2 sts at beg of next row.
Right sleeve only
Cast off 3 sts at beg and dec 1 st at end of next row. 9 sts.
Work 1 row.
Cast off 2 sts at beg and dec 1 st at end of next row. 6 sts.
Rep last 2 rows once more.
Work 1 row.
Both sleeves
Cast off rem 3 sts.

MAKING UP

PRESS as described on the information page.
Join raglan seams using back stitch, or mattress st if preferred.
Neckband
With RS facing, using 4mm (US 6) needles and yarn F, pick up and knit 10 (10: 12: 12: 12) sts up right side of neck, 7 sts from right sleeve, 13 (13: 15: 15: 17) sts from back, 7 sts from left sleeve, then 10 (10: 12: 12: 12) sts down left side of neck. 47 (47: 53: 53: 55) sts.
Beg with a K row, work in rev st st for 4 rows.
Cast off knitwise (on WS).
Front bands (both alike)
With RS facing, using 4mm (US 6) needles and yarn F, pick up and knit 31 (38: 43: 49: 58) sts along one front opening edge, between points 2 rows up from neckband pick-up row and 5 rows up from cast-on edge.
Beg with a K row, work in rev st st for 4 rows.
Cast off knitwise (on WS).
See information page for finishing instructions.

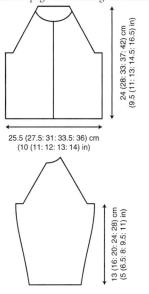

25.5 (27.5: 31: 33.5: 36) cm
(10 (11: 12: 13: 14) in)

24 (28: 33: 37: 42) cm
(9.5 (11: 13: 14.5: 16.5) in)

13 (16: 20: 24: 28) cm
(5 (6.5: 8: 9.5: 11) in)

S<small>OLO</small>

YARN

	1st	2nd	3rd	4th	5th	size
	months		years			
To fit age	0-6	6-12	1-2	2-3	4-5	
To fit chest	41	46	51	56	61	cm
	16	18	20	22	24	in

Rowan Denim

	3	4	5	7	8 x 50gm

(photographed in Tennessee 231)

NEEDLES

1 pair 3¼mm (no 10) (US 3) needles
1 pair 4mm (no 8) (US 6) needles

BUTTONS – 7 x 75324

TENSION

Before washing: 20 sts and 28 rows to 10 cm measured over stocking stitch using 4mm (US 6) needles.

Tension note: **Denim** will shrink in length when washed for the first time. Allowances have been made in the pattern for shrinkage (see size diagram for after washing measurements).

BACK

Cast on 49 (55: 59: 65: 71) sts using 3¼mm (US 3) needles.
Row 1 (RS): K1, *P1, K1, rep from * to end.
Row 2: As row 1.
These 2 rows form moss st.
Work in moss st for a further 4 rows, ending with a WS row.
Change to 4mm (US 6) needles.
Row 1 (RS): P14 (15: 16: 17: 18), K2 (place marker between these 2 sts), P1, K15 (19: 21: 25: 29), P1, K2 (place second marker between these 2 sts), P to end.
Row 2: K14 (15: 16: 17: 18), P2, K1, P15 (19: 21: 25: 29), K1, P2, K to end.
These 2 rows form patt.
Work in patt for a further 2 rows, ending with a WS row.
Next row (shaping row) (RS): P to within 4 sts of first marker, P2tog tbl, P1, K2 (marker is between these sts), P1, M1, K to within 2 sts of

second marker, M1, P1, K2 (marker is between these sts), P1, P2tog, P to end.
Work 3 (5: 9: 11: 15) rows, working increased sts of centre panel in st st.
Rep last 4 (6: 10: 12: 16) rows twice more, then first of these rows (the shaping row) again.
Cont straight until back measures 9.5 (13: 17: 20.5: 25) cm, ending with a WS row.
Shape armholes
Keeping patt correct, cast off 4 sts at beg of next 2 rows. 41 (47: 51: 57: 63) sts.
Work a further 4 (6: 8: 10: 12) rows, ending with a WS row.
Now work in moss st as given for lower edge until armhole measures 14.5 (15.5: 17: 18: 19) cm, ending with a WS row.
Shape shoulders and back neck
Cast off 5 (5: 6: 6: 7) sts at beg of next 2 rows. 31 (37: 39: 45: 49) sts.
Next row (RS): Cast off 5 (5: 6: 6: 7) sts, moss st until there are 8 (10: 9: 11: 11) sts on right needle and turn, leaving rem sts on a holder.
Work each side of neck separately.
Cast off 4 sts at beg of next row.
Cast off rem 4 (6: 5: 7: 7) sts.
With RS facing, rejoin yarn to rem sts, cast off centre 5 (7: 9: 11: 13) sts, moss st to end.
Complete to match first side, reversing shapings.

LEFT FRONT

Cast on 29 (32: 34: 37: 40) sts using 3¼mm (US 3) needles.
Row 1 (RS): *K1, P1, rep from * to last 1 (0: 0: 1: 0) st, K1 (0: 0: 1: 0).
Row 2: K1 (0: 0: 1: 0), *P1, K1, rep from * to end.
These 2 rows form moss st.
Work in moss st for a further 2 rows, ending with a WS row.
Row 5 (RS): Moss st to last 3 sts, yrn, work 2 tog (to make a buttonhole), moss st 1 st.
Row 6: Moss st 5 sts and slip these sts onto a holder, M1, moss st to end. 25 (28: 30: 33: 36) sts.
Change to 4mm (US 6) needles.
Row 1 (RS): P9 (10: 11: 12: 13), K2 (place marker between these 2 sts), P1, moss st 3 sts, P1, K2 (place second marker between these 2 sts), P to end.
Row 2: K7 (9: 10: 12: 14), P2, K1, moss st 3 sts, K1, P2, K to end.
These 2 rows form patt.
Work in patt for a further 6 (8: 12: 14: 18) rows, ending with a WS row.
Next row (shaping row) (RS): P to within 4 sts of first marker, P2tog tbl, P1, K2, P1, M1, moss st to within 2 sts of second marker, M1, P1, K2, P1, P2tog, P to end.
Work 7 (11: 19: 23: 31) rows, working increased sts of centre panel in moss st.
Rep the shaping row once more.
Cont straight until left front matches back to beg of armhole shaping, ending with a WS row.
Shape armhole
Keeping patt correct, cast off 4 sts at beg of next row. 21 (24: 26: 29: 32) sts.
Work a further 5 (7: 9: 11: 13) rows, ending with a WS row.
Now work all sts in moss st as set by central panel until 9 (9: 11: 11: 11) rows less have been worked than on back to start of shoulder shaping, ending with a RS row.
Shape neck
Cast off 3 (4: 4: 5: 6) sts at beg of next row.
18 (20: 22: 24: 26) sts.
Dec 1 st at neck edge of next 3 rows, then on

foll 1 (1: 2: 2: 2) alt rows. 14 (16: 17: 19: 21) sts.
Work 3 rows, ending with a WS row.
Shape shoulder
Cast off 5 (5: 6: 6: 7) sts at beg of next and foll alt row.
Work 1 row. Cast off rem 4 (6: 5: 7: 7) sts.

RIGHT FRONT

Cast on 29 (32: 34: 37: 40) sts using 3¼mm (US 3) needles.
Row 1 (RS): K1 (0: 0: 1: 0), *P1, K1, rep from * to end.
Row 2: *K1, P1, rep from * to last 1 (0: 0: 1: 0) st, K1 (0: 0: 1: 0).
These 2 rows form moss st.
Work in moss st for a further 3 rows, ending with a RS row.
Row 6 (WS): Moss st to last 5 sts, M1 and turn, leaving last 5 sts on a holder. 25 (28: 30: 33: 36) sts.
Change to 4mm (US 6) needles.
Row 1 (RS): P7 (9: 10: 12: 14), K2 (place marker between these 2 sts), P1, moss st 3 sts, P1, K2 (place second marker between these 2 sts), P to end.
Row 2: K9 (10: 11: 12: 13), P2, K1, moss st 3 sts, K1, P2, K to end.
These 2 rows form patt.
Complete to match left front, reversing shapings.

SLEEVES (both alike)

Cast on 29 (31: 33: 35: 37) sts using 3¼mm (US 3) needles.
Work in moss st as given for back for 10 rows, inc 1 st at each end of 9th of these rows and ending with a WS row. 31 (33: 35: 37: 39) sts.
Change to 4mm (US 6) needles.
Beg with a K row, cont in st st, shaping sides by inc 1 st at each end of 3rd (5th: 5th: 5th: 7th) and every foll 4th (6th: 6th: 6th: 8th) row to 45 (37: 43: 61: 45) sts, then on every foll alt (4th: 4th: –: 6th) row until there are 49 (53: 57: –: 65) sts.
Cont straight until sleeve measures 18 (21.5: 26.5: 33.5: 38.5) cm, ending with a WS row.
Cast off.

MAKING UP

DO NOT PRESS.
Join both shoulder seams using back stitch, or mattress st if preferred.
Button band
Slip 5 sts from right front holder onto 3¼mm (US 3) needles and rejoin yarn with WS facing.
Cont in moss st as set until band, when slightly stretched, fits up right front opening edge to neck shaping, ending with a WS row.

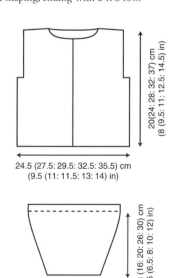

24.5 (27.5: 29.5: 32.5: 35.5) cm
(9.5 (11: 11.5: 13: 14) in)

20(24: 28: 32: 37) cm
(8 (9.5: 11: 12.5: 14.5) in)

13 (16: 20: 26: 30) cm
(5 (6.5: 8: 10: 12) in)

Cast off.

Slip st band in place.

Mark positions for 5 buttons on this band – first to come level with buttonhole already worked in left front, last to come 1 cm below neck shaping and rem 3 buttons evenly spaced between.

Buttonhole band

Slip 5 sts from left front holder onto 3¼mm (US 3) needles and rejoin yarn with RS facing. Cont in moss st as set until band, when slightly stretched, fits up left front opening edge to neck shaping, ending with a WS row and with the addition of a further 4 buttonholes worked to correspond with positions marked for buttons as folls:

Buttonhole row (RS): Moss st 2 sts, yrn, work 2 tog (to make a buttonhole), moss st 1 st. When band is complete, cast off.

Slip st band in place.

Collar

Cast on 45 (49: 55: 59: 63) sts using 3¼mm (US 3) needles.

Work in moss st as given for back for 6 (7: 7: 8: 8) cm. Cast off in moss st.

Pocket flaps (make 2)

Cast on 17 sts using 3¼mm (US 3) needles.

Work in moss st as given for back for 8 rows. Dec 1 st at each end of next 4 rows. 9 sts. Cast off in moss st.

Machine wash all pieces before completion.

Sew cast-on edge of pocket flaps to fronts level with start of moss st yoke and centrally over centre moss st panel. Fold flap down and secure by sewing on a button through both layers. Sew cast-on edge of collar to neck edge, positioning ends of collar halfway across top of bands.

See information page for finishing instructions, setting in sleeves using the square set-in method.

BOB

YARN

		1st	2nd	3rd	4th	5th	size
		months			years		
To fit age		0-6	6-12	1-2	2-3	4-5	
To fit chest		41	46	51	56	61	cm
		16	18	20	22	24	in
Rowan All Seasons Cotton							
A Limedrop	197	1	1	1	2	2	x 50gm
B Jazz	185	1	1	1	2	2	x 50gm
C Dp Marine	176	1	1	1	1	1	x 50gm
D Dusky	164	1	1	1	1	1	x 50gm
E Sea View	166	1	1	1	1	1	x 50gm
F True Blue	165	1	1	1	1	1	x 50gm
G Dim	201	1	1	1	1	1	x 50gm

NEEDLES

1 pair 4mm (no 8) (US 6) needles
1 pair 4½mm (no 7) (US 7) needles
1 pair 5mm (no 6) (US 8) needles

TENSION

17 sts and 24 rows to 10 cm measured over stocking stitch using 5mm (US 8) needles.

STRIPE SEQUENCE

Beg with a K row, work in st st as folls:

Rows 1 and 2: Using yarn A.
Rows 3 and 4: Using yarn B.
Rows 5 and 6: Using yarn C.
Rows 7 and 8: Using yarn D.
Rows 9 and 10: Using yarn E.
Rows 11 and 12: Using yarn G.

Rows 13 and 14: Using yarn D.
Rows 15 and 16: Using yarn F.
Rows 17 and 18: Using yarn A.
Rows 19 and 20: Using yarn C.
Rows 21 and 22: Using yarn B.
Rows 23 and 24: Using yarn A.
Rows 25 and 26: Using yarn B.
Rows 27 and 28: Using yarn F.
Rows 29 and 30: Using yarn E.
Rows 31 and 32: Using yarn D.
Rows 33 and 34: Using yarn A.
Rows 35 and 36: Using yarn G.
Rows 37 and 38: Using yarn C.
Rows 39 and 40: Using yarn A.
Rows 41 and 42: Using yarn B.
Rows 43 and 44: Using yarn D.
Rows 45 and 46: Using yarn E.
Rows 47 and 48: Using yarn F.
Rows 49 and 50: Using yarn C.
Rows 51 and 52: Using yarn B.
Rows 53 and 54: Using yarn A.
Rows 55 and 56: Using yarn F.
Rows 57 and 58: Using yarn G.
Rows 59 and 60: Using yarn D.
Rows 61 and 62: Using yarn E.

These 62 rows form stripe sequence.

BACK

Cast on 39 (43: 47: 53: 57) sts using 4½mm (US 7) needles and yarn A.

Row 1 (RS): K1 (3: 0: 3: 0), ★P2, K3, rep from ★ to last 3 (0: 2: 0: 2) sts, P2 (0: 2: 0: 2), K1 (0: 0: 0: 0).

Row 2: P1 (3: 0: 3: 0), ★K2, P3, rep from ★ to last 3 (0: 2: 0: 2) sts, K2 (0: 2: 0: 2), P1 (0: 0: 0: 0).

These 2 rows form rib.

Work in rib for a further 4 rows, ending with a WS row.

Change to 5mm (US 8) needles.

Beg with a K row and row 1, cont in st st in stripe sequence as detailed above until back measures 12 (15: 18: 21: 25) cm, ending with a WS row.

Shape armholes

Keeping stripes correct, cast off 3 sts at beg of next 2 rows. 33 (37: 41: 47: 51) sts.

Dec 1 st at each end of next 3 rows. 27 (31: 35: 41: 45) sts.

Cont straight until armhole measures 11 (12: 13: 14: 15) cm, ending with a WS row.

Shape shoulders and back neck

Next row (RS): Cast off 2 (3: 3: 4: 5) sts, K until there are 6 (6: 7: 8: 8) sts on right needle and turn, leaving rem sts on a holder.

Work each side of neck separately.

Cast off 3 sts at beg of next row.

Cast off rem 3 (3: 4: 5: 5) sts.

With RS facing, slip centre 11 (13: 15: 17: 19) sts onto a holder, rejoin appropriate yarn to rem sts, K to end.

Complete to match first side, reversing shapings.

FRONT

Work as given for back until 10 (10: 12: 12: 12) rows less have been worked than on back to start of shoulder shaping, ending with a WS row.

Shape neck

Next row (RS): K8 (9: 11: 13: 14) and turn, leaving rem sts on a holder.

Work each side of neck separately.

Dec 1 st at neck edge of next 2 rows, then on foll 1 (1: 2: 2: 2) alt rows. 5 (6: 7: 9: 10) sts.

Work 5 rows, ending with a WS row.

Shape shoulder

Cast off 2 (3: 3: 4: 5) sts at beg of next row.

Work 1 row.

Cast off rem 3 (3: 4: 5: 5) sts.

With RS facing, slip centre 11 (13: 13: 15: 17) sts onto a holder, rejoin appropriate yarn to rem sts, K to end.

Complete to match first side, reversing shapings.

MAKING UP

PRESS as described on the information page.

Join right shoulder seam using back stitch, or mattress st if preferred.

Neckband

With RS facing, using 4½mm (US 7) needles and yarn B, pick up and knit 10 (10: 12: 12: 13) sts down left side of front neck, knit across 11 (13: 13: 15: 17) sts from front holder, pick up and knit 10 (10: 12: 12: 13) sts up right side of front neck, and 3 sts down right side of back neck, knit across 11 (13: 15: 17: 19) sts from back holder dec 1 (0: 1: 0: 1) st at centre, pick up and knit 3 sts up left side of back neck. 47 (52: 57: 62: 67) sts.

Row 1 (WS): K2, ★P3, K2, rep from ★ to end.
Row 2: P2, ★K3, P2, rep from ★ to end.
Row 3: As row 1.

Cast off **loosely** in rib.

Join left shoulder and neckband seam.

Armhole borders (both alike)

With RS facing, using 4½mm (US 7) needles and yarn B, pick up and knit 47 (52: 57: 62: 67) sts evenly around armhole edge.

Work rows 1 to 3 as given for neckband.

Cast off **loosely** in rib.

See information page for finishing instructions.

23 (25.5: 27.5: 31: 33.5) cm
(9 (10: 11: 12: 13) in)

23 (27: 31: 35: 40) cm
(9 (10.5: 12: 14: 15.5) in)

D AYDREAM

YARN

	1st	2nd	3rd	
	months		years	
To fit age	0-6	6-12	1-2	
To fit chest	41	46	51	cm
	16	18	20	in

Rowan Cotton Glace

| | 3 | 3 | 4 | x 50gm |

(photographed in Glee 799)

NEEDLES

1 pair 2³/₄mm (no 12) (US 2) needles
1 pair 3mm (no 11) (US 2/3) needles
1 pair 3¹/₄mm (no 10) (US 3) needles

BUTTONS – 3 x 75333

RIBBON – 1 m of narrow satin ribbon

TENSION

23 sts and 32 rows to 10 cm measured over stocking stitch using 3¹/₄mm (US 3) needles.

BACK

Cast on 65 (75: 81) sts using 3mm (US 2/3) needles.
Row 1 (RS): Purl.
Row 2: Knit.
Row 3: K2 (1: 4), (K2tog, K4, yfwd) 1 (0: 0) times, *K1, yfwd, K4, sl 2, K1, p2sso, K4, yfwd, rep from * to last 9 (2: 5) sts, (K1, yfwd, K4, sl 1, K1, psso) 1 (0: 0) times, K2 (2: 5).
Row 4: Purl.
Row 5: K2 (1: 4), (K2tog, K3, yfwd, K1) 1 (0: 0) times, *K2, yfwd, K3, sl 2, K1, p2sso, K3, yfwd, K1, rep from * to last 9 (2: 5) sts, (K2, yfwd, K3, sl 1, K1, psso) 1 (0: 0) times, K2 (2: 5).
Row 6: Purl.
Row 7: K2 (1: 4), (K2tog, K2, yfwd, K2) 1 (0: 0) times, *K3, yfwd, K2, sl 2, K1, p2sso, K2, yfwd, K2, rep from * to last 9 (2: 5) sts, (K3, yfwd, K2, sl 1, K1, psso) 1 (0: 0) times, K2 (2: 5).
Row 8: Purl.
Row 9: K2 (1: 4), (K2tog, K1, yfwd, K3) 1 (0: 0) times, *K4, yfwd, K1, sl 2, K1, p2sso, K1, yfwd, K3, rep from * to last 9 (2: 5) sts, (K4, yfwd, K1, sl 1, K1, psso) 1 (0: 0) times, K2 (2: 5).
Row 10: Purl.

Row 11: K2 (1: 4), (K2tog, yfwd, K4) 1 (0: 0) times, *K5, yfwd, sl 2, K1, p2sso, yfwd, K4, rep from * to last 9 (2: 5) sts, (K5, yfwd, sl 1, K1, psso) 1 (0: 0) times, K2 (2: 5).
Row 12: Purl.
Row 13: K8 (1: 4), *K5, sl 2, K1, p2sso, K4, rep from * to last 9 (2: 5) sts, K9 (2: 5). 57 (63: 69) sts.
Change to 3¹/₄mm (US 3) needles.
Beg with a **purl** row, work in st st until back measures 11 (14: 17) cm, ending with a WS row.
Next row (eyelet row)(RS): K1 (4: 3), (K2tog, yfwd, K2) 6 (6: 7) times, K2tog, yfwd, K3, yfwd, K2tog, (K2, yfwd, K2tog) 6 (6: 7) times, K1 (4: 3).
Work 3 rows, ending with a WS row.
Shape raglan armholes
Cast off 4 sts at beg of next 2 rows. 49 (55: 61) sts.
Next row (RS): P1, K1, K2tog, yfwd, K2tog, K to last 6 sts, K2tog tbl, yfwd, K2tog tbl, K1, P1.
Next row: K1, P to last st, K1.
Working all raglan decreases and eyelets as set by last 2 rows, dec 1 st at each end of next and every foll alt row until 19 (21: 23) sts rem.
Work 1 row, ending with a WS row. Cast off.

LEFT FRONT

Cast on 33 (38: 41) sts using 3mm (US 2/3) needles.
Row 1 (RS): Purl.
Row 2: Knit.
Row 3: K2 (1: 4), (K2tog, K4, yfwd) 1 (0: 0) times, *K1, yfwd, K4, sl 2, K1, p2sso, K4, yfwd, rep from * to last st, K1.
Row 4: Purl.
Row 5: K2 (1: 4), (K2tog, K3, yfwd, K1) 1 (0: 0) times, *K2, yfwd, K3, sl 2, K1, p2sso, K3, yfwd, K1, rep from * to last st, K1.
Row 6: Purl.
Row 7: K2 (1: 4), (K2tog, K2, yfwd, K2) 1 (0: 0) times, *K3, yfwd, K2, sl 2, K1, p2sso, K2, yfwd, K2, rep from * to last st, K1.
Row 8: Purl.
Row 9: K2 (1: 4), (K2tog, K1, yfwd, K3) 1 (0: 0) times, *K4, yfwd, K1, sl 2, K1, p2sso, K1, yfwd, K3, rep from * to last st, K1.
Row 10: Purl.
Row 11: K2 (1: 4), (K2tog, yfwd, K4) 1 (0: 0) times, *K5, yfwd, sl 2, K1, p2sso, yfwd, K4, rep from * to last st, K1.
Row 12: Purl.
Row 13: K8 (1: 4), *K5, sl 2, K1, p2sso, K4, rep from * to last st, K1. 29 (32: 35) sts.
Change to 3¹/₄mm (US 3) needles.
Beg with a **purl** row, work in st st until left front measures 11 (14: 17) cm, ending with a WS row.
Next row (eyelet row) (RS): K1 (4: 3), (K2tog, yfwd, K2) 7 (7: 8) times.
Work 3 rows, ending with a WS row.
Shape raglan armhole
Cast off 4 sts at beg of next row. 25 (28: 31) sts.
Work 1 row.
Next row (RS): P1, K1, K2tog, yfwd, K2tog, K to end.
Next row: P to last st, K1.
Working all raglan decreases and eyelets as set by last 2 rows, dec 1 st at raglan armhole edge of next and every foll alt row until 19 (20: 22) sts rem.
Work 1 (0: 1) row, ending with a WS (RS: WS) row.
Shape front slope
Dec 1 st at front slope edge of next 8 (9: 10) rows **and at same time** dec 1 st and work eyelets as before at raglan armhole edge of next (2nd: next) and every foll alt row. 7 sts.
Next row (RS): P1, K1, K2tog, yfwd, K3tog. 5 sts.

Next row: P2tog, P2, K1.
Next row: P1, K3tog.
Next row: P1, K1.
Next row: K2tog and fasten off.

RIGHT FRONT

Cast on 33 (38: 41) sts using 3mm (US 2/3) needles.
Row 1 (RS): Purl.
Row 2: Knit.
Row 3: *K1, yfwd, K4, sl 2, K1, p2sso, K4, yfwd, rep from * to last 9 (2: 5) sts, (K1, yfwd, K4, sl 1, K1, psso) 1 (0: 0) times, K2 (2: 5).
Row 4: Purl.
Row 5: *K2, yfwd, K3, sl 2, K1, p2sso, K3, yfwd, K1, rep from * to last 9 (2: 5) sts, (K2, yfwd, K3, sl 1, K1, psso) 1 (0: 0) times, K2 (2: 5).
Row 6: Purl.
Row 7: *K3, yfwd, K2, sl 2, K1, p2sso, K2, yfwd, K2, rep from * to last 9 (2: 5) sts, (K3, yfwd, K2, sl 1, K1, psso) 1 (0: 0) times, K2 (2: 5).
Row 8: Purl.
Row 9: *K4, yfwd, K1, sl 2, K1, p2sso, K1, yfwd, K3, rep from * to last 9 (2: 5) sts, (K4, yfwd, K1, sl 1, K1, psso) 1 (0: 0) times, K2 (2: 5).
Row 10: Purl.
Row 11: *K5, yfwd, sl 2, K1, p2sso, yfwd, K4, rep from * to last 9 (2: 5) sts, (K5, yfwd, sl 1, K1, psso) 1 (0: 0) times, K2 (2: 5).
Row 12: Purl.
Row 13: *K5, sl 2, K1, p2sso, K4, rep from * to last 9 (2: 5) sts, K9 (2: 5). 29 (32: 35) sts.
Change to 3¹/₄mm (US 3) needles.
Beg with a **purl** row, work in st st until right front measures 11 (14: 17) cm, ending with a WS row.
Next row (eyelet row) (RS): (K2, yfwd, K2tog) 7 (7: 8) times, K1 (4: 3).
Complete to match left front, reversing shapings.

SLEEVES

Cast on 33 (35: 37) sts using 2³/₄mm (US 2) needles.
Row 1 (RS): Purl.
Row 2: Knit.
Change to 3¹/₄mm (US 3) needles.
Beg with a K row, work in st st, shaping sides by inc 1 st at each end of next (3rd: 3rd) and every foll alt (4th: 4th) row to 37 (51: 49) sts, then on every foll 4th (6th: 6th) row until there are 49 (53: 57) sts.

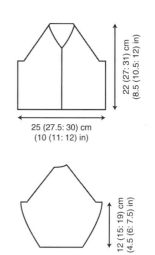

25 (27.5: 30) cm
(10 (11: 12) in)

22 (27: 31) cm
(8.5 (10.5: 12) in)

12 (15: 19) cm
(4.5 (6: 7.5) in)

Cont straight until sleeve measures 12 (15: 19) cm, ending with a WS row.

Shape raglan

Cast off 4 sts at beg of next 2 rows.

41 (45: 49) sts.

Working all raglan decreases and eyelets as given for back, dec 1 st at each end of next and every foll alt row until 17 sts rem.

Work 1 row, ending with a WS row.

Left sleeve only

Next row (RS): P1, K1, K2tog, yfwd, K2tog, K5, K2tog tbl, yfwd, K2tog tbl, K1, P1. 15 sts.

Next row: Cast off 3 sts, P to last st, K1. 12 sts.

Next row: P1, K1, K2tog, yfwd, K2tog, to end. 11 sts.

Next row: Cast off 3 sts, P to last st, K1. 8 sts.

Rep last 2 rows once more.

Right sleeve only

Next row (RS): Cast off 4 sts, K to last 6 sts,

K2tog tbl, yfwd, K2tog tbl, K1, P1. 12 sts.

Next row: K1, P to end.

Next row: Cast off 3 sts, K to last 6 sts, K2tog tbl, yfwd, K2tog tbl, K1, P1. 8 sts.

Next row: K1, P to end.

Next row: Cast off 4 sts, K to last st, P1. 4 sts.

Next row: K1, P3.

Both sleeves

Cast off rem 4 sts.

MAKING UP

PRESS as described on the information page.

Join raglan seams using back stitch, or mattress st if preferred.

Mark positions for 3 buttonholes along right front opening edge – first to come level with eyelet row, last to come just below start of front slope shaping and rem buttonhole halfway between these 2.

Front band

With RS facing and using 2¾mm (US 2) needles, starting and ending at cast-on edges, pick up and knit 40 (51: 63) sts up right front opening edge to start of front slope shaping, 12 (13: 14) sts up right front slope, 11 sts from right sleeve, 19 (21: 23) sts from back, 11 sts from left sleeve, 12 (13: 14) sts down left front slope to start of front slope shaping, then 40 (51: 63) sts down left front opening edge. 145 (171: 199) sts.

Row 1 (WS): Knit.

Row 2: P to first marker, (yrn, P2tog, P to next marker) twice, yrn, P2tog, P to end.

Row 3: Knit.

Cast off purlwise (on RS).

See information page for finishing instructions. Thread ribbon in and out of eyelet row and tie in bow at front.

LOLA

YARN

Rowan All Seasons Cotton

		small	medium	large		
A	Kiss	175	1	1	1	x 50gm
B	Valour	181	1	1	1	x 50gm

Oddment of yarn C (Jaunty 183) for flower centre

NEEDLES

1 pair 4mm (no 8) (US 6) needles
1 pair 5mm (no 6) (US 8) needles

TENSION

17 sts and 24 rows to 10 cm measured over stocking stitch using 5mm (US 8) needles.

MEASUREMENTS

Finished hat measures approx 38 (42: 47) cm, 15 (16½: 18½) in, around head.

HAT

Cast on 65 (73: 81) sts using 4mm (US 6) needles and yarn A.

Work in garter st for 6 rows, ending with a WS row.

Change to 5mm (US 8) needles.

Break off yarn A and join in yarn B.

Beg with a K row, work in st st until hat measures 11 (12: 13) cm, ending with a WS row.

Shape top

Large size only

Row 1 (RS): (K8, K2tog) 8 times, K1. 73 sts.

Work 1 row.

Medium and large size only

Next row (RS): (K7, K2tog) 8 times, K1. 65 sts.

Work 1 row.

All sizes

Next row (RS): (K6, K2tog) 8 times, K1. 57 sts.

Work 1 row.

Next row: (K5, K2tog) 8 times, K1. 49 sts.

Work 1 row.

Next row: (K4, K2tog) 8 times, K1. 41 sts.

Work 1 row.

Next row: (K3, K2tog) 8 times, K1. 33 sts.

Work 1 row.

Next row: (K2, K2tog) 8 times, K1. 25 sts.

Work 1 row.

Next row: (K1, K2tog) 8 times, K1. 17 sts.

Work 1 row.

Next row: (K2tog) 8 times, K1. 9 sts.

Work 1 row.

Break yarn and thread through rem 9 sts.

Pull up tight and fasten off securely.

Join back seam.

FLOWER

Cast on 57 sts using 4mm (US 6) needles and yarn A.

Row 1 (WS): Purl.

Break off yarn A and join in yarn C.

Row 2: K2, *K1 and slip this st back onto left needle, lift the next 8 sts on left needle over this st and off needle, (yfwd) twice, K first st again, K2, rep from * to end.

Row 3: K1, *P2tog, (K1, K1 tbl) into double (yfwd) of previous row, P1, rep from * to last st, K1.

Row 4: Knit.

Break yarn and thread through rem sts.

Pull up tight and fasten off securely.

Join row end edges.

Make another piece using yarn A throughout.

Lay this flower on top of other flower and attach centres of both flowers to hat as in photograph.

SNUFFLE

YARN

Rowan Big Wool

	S/M	M/L		
	2	2	x	100gm

(photographed in White Hot 001)

NEEDLES

1 pair 12mm (US 17) needles

TENSION

7 sts and 13 rows to 10 cm measured over garter stitch using 12mm (US 17) needles.

MEASUREMENTS

Finished scarf measures 13 (16) cm, 5 (6½) in, wide and 122 (137) cm, 48 (54) in, long excluding fringe.

SCARF

Cast on 9 (11) sts using 12mm (US 17) needles.

Work in garter st until scarf measures 122 (137) cm, ending with a WS row. Cast off.

Cut 20 cm lengths of yarn and knot groups of 4 of these lengths through ends of scarf to form fringe.

LITTLE TREES

YARN

	1st	2nd	3rd	4th	5th	size
	months		years			
To fit age	0-6	6-12	1-2	2-3	4-5	
To fit chest	41	46	51	56	61	cm
	16	18	20	22	24	in
Rowan Wool Cotton						
A Misty	903 1	1	1	2	2	x 50gm
B Antique	900 1	1	1	1	1	x 50gm
C Camel	945 1	1	1	1	1	x 50gm
D Dpst Olive	907 1	1	1	1	1	x 50gm
E Clear	914 2	3	3	4	4	x 50gm

NEEDLES

1 pair 3¼mm (no 10) (US 3) needles
1 pair 4mm (no 8) (US 6) needles

BUTTONS – 5 x 75315

TENSION

22 sts and 30 rows to 10 cm measured over
stocking stitch using 4mm (US 6) needles.

BACK

Cast on 49 (55: 55: 61: 67) sts using 3¼mm
(US 3) needles and yarn A.
Work in garter st for 8 rows, ending with a WS
row.
Change to 4mm (US 6) needles.
Using the **intarsia** technique as described on
the information page, starting and ending rows
as indicated, cont in patt from chart for back,
which is worked entirely in st st beg with a
K row, as folls:
(**Note**: when all 40 rows of chart have been
worked, complete back using yarn E only.)
3rd, 4th and 5th sizes
Inc 1 st at each end of 3rd and every foll 10th
row until there are – (-: 61: 67: 73) sts.
All sizes
Cont straight until back measures 9 (11: 13: 15:
19) cm, ending with a WS row.
Shape armholes
Keeping chart correct, cast off 5 sts at beg of
next 2 rows. 39 (45: 51: 57: 63) sts.
Cont straight until armhole measures 11 (12: 13:
14: 15) cm, ending with a WS row.

Shape shoulders and back neck

Cast off 4 (5: 5: 6: 7) sts at beg of next 2 rows.
31 (35: 41: 45: 49) sts.
Next row (RS): Cast off 4 (5: 5: 6: 7) sts, K until
there are 7 (8: 10: 11: 11) sts on right needle and
turn, leaving rem sts on a holder.
Work each side of neck separately.
Cast off 4 sts at beg of next row.
Cast off rem 3 (4: 6: 7: 7) sts.
With RS facing, rejoin yarn to rem sts, cast off
centre 9 (9: 11: 11: 13) sts, K to end.
Complete to match first side, reversing shapings.

LEFT FRONT

Cast on 25 (28: 28: 31: 34) sts using 3¼mm
(US 3) needles and yarn A.

Work in garter st for 8 rows, ending with a WS
row.
Change to 4mm (US 6) needles.
Starting and ending rows as indicated, cont in
patt from chart for left front as folls:
3rd, 4th and 5th sizes
Inc 1 st at beg of 3rd and every foll 10th row
until there are – (-: 31: 34: 37) sts.
All sizes
Cont straight until left front matches back to
beg of armhole shaping, ending with a WS row.
Shape armhole
Keeping chart correct, cast off 5 sts at beg of
next row. 20 (23: 26: 29: 32) sts.
Cont straight until armhole measures 4 (5: 5: 6:
6) cm, ending with a WS row.

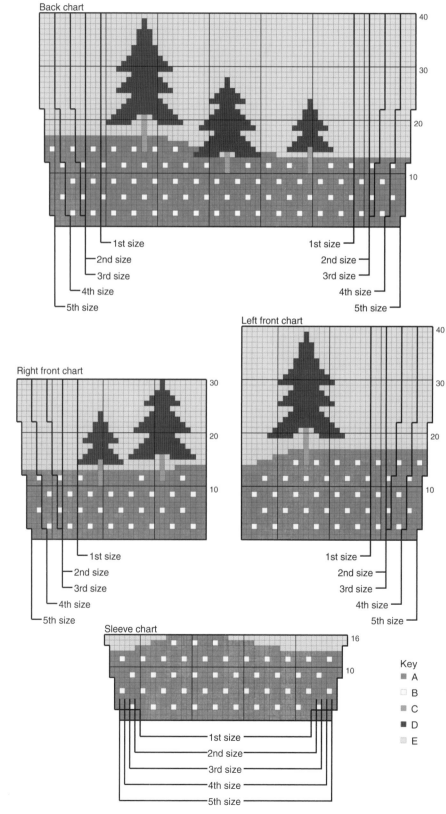

Back chart

1st size
2nd size
3rd size
4th size
5th size

Right front chart

1st size
2nd size
3rd size
4th size
5th size

Left front chart

1st size
2nd size
3rd size
4th size
5th size

Sleeve chart

1st size
2nd size
3rd size
4th size
5th size

Key
■ A
□ B
▨ C
■ D
▨ E

Shape front slope

Dec 1 st at end of next and every foll alt row until 11 (14: 16: 19: 21) sts rem.

Cont straight until left front matches back to start of shoulder shaping, ending with a WS row.

Shape shoulder

Cast off 4 (5: 5: 6: 7) sts at beg of next and foll alt row.

Work 1 row.

Cast off rem 3 (4: 6: 7: 7) sts.

RIGHT FRONT

Cast on 25 (28: 28: 31: 34) sts using 3¼mm (US 3) needles and yarn A.

Work in garter st for 8 rows, end with a WS row.

Change to 4mm (US 6) needles.

Starting and ending rows as indicated, cont in patt from chart for right front as folls:

3rd, 4th and 5th sizes

Inc 1 st at end of 3rd and every foll 10th row until there are – (–: 31: 34: 37) sts.

All sizes

Complete to match left front, reversing shapings.

SLEEVES (both alike)

Cast on 33 (35: 37: 39: 41) sts using 3¼mm (US 3) needles and yarn A.

Work in garter st for 8 rows, end with a WS row.

Change to 4mm (US 6) needles.

Starting and ending rows as indicated, cont in patt from chart for sleeve as folls:

Inc 1 st at each end of 3rd and every foll 4th (4th: 4th: 6th: 6th) row to 39 (45: 51: 43: 51) sts, then on every foll alt (alt: alt: 4th: 4th) row until there are 49 (53: 57: 61: 65) sts.

Cont straight until sleeve measures 13 (15: 18: 23: 27) cm, ending with a WS row. Cast off.

MAKING UP

PRESS as described on the information page. Join both shoulder seams using back stitch, or mattress st if preferred.

Button band and collar

Cast on 5 sts using 3¼mm (US 3) needles and yarn E.

Cont in garter st until band, when slightly stretched, fits up front opening edge to start of front slope shaping, ending at inner edge (edge that will be sewn to front).

Shape for collar

Inc 1 st at inner edge of next 15 rows, then on every foll alt row until there are 26 sts.

Cont straight until collar, unstretched, fits up front slope and across to centre back neck, ending at inner edge.

Cast off 6 sts at beg of next and foll 2 alt rows.

Work 1 row. Cast off rem 8 sts.

Slip stitch button band in place. Mark positions for 5 buttons on this band – first to come 1.5 cm up from cast-on edge, last to come 1.5 cm below start of front slope shaping and rem 3 buttons evenly spaced between.

Buttonhole band and collar

Work to match button band and collar, reversing shapings and with the addition of 5 buttonholes worked to correspond with positions marked for buttons as folls:

Buttonhole row (RS): K1, K2tog, yfwd (to make a buttonhole), K2.

Join cast-off ends of collar, then slip stitch bands and collar in place.

See information page for finishing instructions, setting in sleeves using the square set-in method.

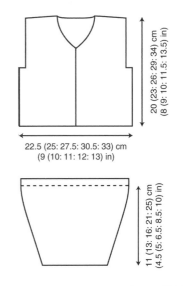

20 (23: 26: 29: 34) cm
(8: 9: 10: 11.5: 13.5) in

22.5 (25: 27.5: 30.5: 33) cm
(9: 10: 11: 12: 13) in

11 (13: 16: 21: 25) cm
(4.5: 5: 6.5: 8.5: 10) in

DESIGN NUMBER 26

COTTON CANDY

YARN

	1st	2nd	3rd	4th	5th size
		months		years	
To fit age	0-6	6-12	1-2	2-3	4-5
To fit chest	41	46	51	56	61 cm
	16	18	20	22	24 in
Rowan Denim					
A Tennessee 231	2	3	3	4	5 x 50gm
B Ecru 324	2	2	3	3	4 x 50gm

NEEDLES

1 pair 3¼mm (no 10) (US 3) needles
1 pair 4mm (no 8) (US 6) needles

BUTTONS – 5 x 75320

TENSION

Before washing: 20 sts and 28 rows to 10 cm measured over stocking stitch using 4mm (US 6) needles.

Tension Note

Denim will shrink in length when washed for the first time. Allowances have been made in the pattern for shrinkage (see size diagram for after washing measurements).

BACK

Cast on 47 (53: 57: 63: 69) sts using 3¼mm (US 3) needles and yarn A.

Row 1 (RS): P1, *K1, P1, rep from * to end.

Row 2: As row 1.

These 2 rows form moss st.

Work in moss st for a further 6 rows, ending with a WS row.

Change to 4mm (US 6) needles.

Beg with a K row, cont in st st as folls:

Using yarn A, work 2 rows.

Join in yarn B.

Using yarn B, work 2 rows.

Last 4 rows form striped st st.

Cont in striped st st until back measures 12 (17: 20.5: 24: 29) cm, ending with a WS row.

Shape raglan armholes

Keeping stripes correct, cast off 4 sts at beg of next 2 rows. 39 (45: 49: 55: 61) sts.

1st, 2nd, 3rd and 4th sizes

Dec 1 st at each end of next and foll 4th row. 35 (41: 45: 51: –) sts.

Work 3 (1: 1: 1: –) rows.

All sizes

Dec 1 st at each end of next and every foll alt row until 13 (15: 17: 19: 21) sts rem.

Work 1 row, ending with a WS row.

Cast off.

POCKET LININGS (make 2)

Cast on 14 (15: 16: 17: 18) sts using 4mm (US 6) needles and yarn A.

Beg with a K row and 2 rows using yarn A, work in striped st st as given for back for 12 (12: 16: 16: 20) rows.

Break yarn and leave sts on a holder.

LEFT FRONT

Cast on 29 (32: 34: 37: 40) sts using 3¼mm (US 3) needles and yarn A.

Row 1 (RS): *P1, K1, rep from * to last 1 (0: 0: 1: 0) st, P1 (0: 0: 1: 0).

Row 2: P1 (0: 0: 1: 0), *K1, P1, rep from * to end.

These 2 rows form moss st.

Work in moss st for a further 5 rows, ending with a RS row.

Row 8 (WS): Moss st 6 sts and slip these sts onto a holder, M1, moss st to end. 24 (27: 29: 32: 35) sts.

Change to 4mm (US 6) needles.

Beg with a K row and 2 rows using yarn A, work in striped st st as given for back for 20 (20: 24: 24: 28) rows, ending with a WS row.

Place pocket

Next row (RS): K3 (4: 5: 6: 7), slip next 14 (15: 16: 17: 18) sts onto a holder and, in their place, K across 14 (15: 16: 17: 18) sts of first pocket lining, K7 (8: 8: 9: 10).

Cont straight until left front matches back to beg of raglan armhole shaping, ending with a WS row.

Shape raglan armhole

Keeping stripes correct, cast off 4 sts at beg of next row. 20 (23: 25: 28: 31) sts.

Work 1 row.

1st, 2nd, 3rd and 4th sizes

Dec 1 st at raglan armhole edge of next and foll 4th row. 18 (21: 23: 26: –) sts.

Work 3 (1: 1: 1: –) rows.

71

All sizes

Dec 1 st at raglan armhole edge of next and every foll alt row until 13 (14: 16: 17: 18) sts rem, ending with a RS row.

Shape neck

Keeping stripes correct, cast off 3 (4: 4: 5: 6) sts at beg of next row. 10 (10: 12: 12: 12) sts.

Dec 1 st at neck edge of next 5 rows, then on foll 0 (0: 1: 1: 1) alt row **and at same time** dec 1 st at raglan armhole edge of next and every foll alt row. 2 sts.

Work 1 row, ending with a WS row.

Next row: K2tog and fasten off.

RIGHT FRONT

Cast on 29 (32: 34: 37: 40) sts using 3¼mm (US 3) needles and yarn A.

Row 1 (RS): P1 (0: 0: 1: 0), ★K1, P1, rep from ★ to end.

Row 2: ★P1, K1, rep from ★ to last 1 (0: 0: 1: 0) st, P1 (0: 0: 1: 0).

These 2 rows form moss st.

Work in moss st for a further 2 rows, ending with a WS row.

Row 5 (RS): Moss st 1 st, work 2 tog, yrn (to make a buttonhole), moss st to end.

Work in moss st for a further 2 rows, ending with a RS row.

Row 8 (WS): Moss st to last 6 sts, M1 and turn, leaving last 6 sts on a holder. 24 (27: 29: 32: 35) sts.

Change to 4mm (US 6) needles.

Beg with a K row and 2 rows using yarn A, work in striped st st as given for back for 20 (20: 24: 24: 28) rows, ending with a WS row.

Place pocket

Next row (RS): K7 (8: 8: 9: 10), slip next 14 (15: 16: 17: 18) sts onto a holder and, in their place, K across 14 (15: 16: 17: 18) sts of second pocket lining, K3 (4: 5: 6: 7).

Complete to match left front, reversing shapings.

SLEEVES

Cast on 27 (29: 31: 33: 35) sts using 3¼mm (US 3) needles and yarn A.

Work in moss st as given for back for 8 rows, ending with a WS row.

Change to 4mm (US 6) needles.

Beg with a K row and 2 rows using yarn A, cont in striped st st as given for back, shaping sides by inc 1 st at each end of 3rd and every foll 4th (4th: 6th: 6th: 8th) row to 33 (45: 41: 51: 47) sts, then on every foll alt (alt: 4th: 4th: 6th) row until there are 45 (47: 49: 53: 55) sts.

Cont straight until sleeve measures 14.5 (18: 23: 27.5: 32.5) cm, ending with same stripe row as on back to beg of raglan armhole shaping and a WS row.

Shape raglan

Keeping stripes correct, cast off 4 sts at beg of next 2 rows. 37 (39: 41: 45: 47) sts.

Dec 1 st at each end of next and every foll alt row until 13 sts rem.

Work 1 row, ending with a WS row.

Left sleeve only

Dec 1 st at each end of next row. 11 sts.

Cast off 2 sts at beg of next row, then dec 1 st at beg of foll row. 8 sts.

Rep last 2 rows once more. 5 sts.

Cast off 2 sts at beg of next row.

Right sleeve only

Cast off 3 sts at beg and dec 1 st at end of next row. 9 sts.

Work 1 row.

Cast off 2 sts at beg and dec 1 st at end of next row. 6 sts.

Rep last 2 rows once more.

Work 1 row.

Both sleeves

Cast off rem 3 sts.

MAKING UP

DO NOT PRESS.

Join raglan seams using back stitch, or mattress st if preferred.

Button band

Slip 6 sts from left front holder onto 3¼mm (US 3) needles and rejoin yarn A with RS facing.

Cont in moss st as set until band, when slightly stretched, fits up left front opening edge to neck shaping, ending with a WS row.

Cast off.

Slip st band in place.

Mark positions for 5 buttons on this band – first to come level with buttonhole already worked in right front, last to come 1.5 cm below neck shaping and rem 3 buttons evenly spaced between.

Buttonhole band

Slip 6 sts from right front holder onto 3¼mm (US 3) needles and rejoin yarn A with WS facing.

Cont in moss st as set until band, when slightly stretched, fits up right front opening edge to neck shaping, ending with a WS row and with the addition of a further 4 buttonholes worked to correspond with positions marked for buttons as folls:

Buttonhole row (RS): Moss st 1 st, work 2 tog, yrn (to make a buttonhole), moss st 3 sts.

When band is complete, cast off.

Slip st band in place.

Collar

Cast on 45 (49: 55: 59: 63) sts using 3¼mm (US 3) needles and yarn A.

Work in moss st as given for back for 7.5 (8.5: 8.5: 9.5: 9.5) cm. Cast off in moss st.

Pocket borders (both alike)

Slip 14 (15: 16: 17: 18) sts from pocket holder onto 3¼mm (US 3) needles, rejoin yarn A with RS facing and work in moss st for 4 rows.

Cast off in moss st.

Machine wash all pieces before completion.

See information page for finishing instructions.

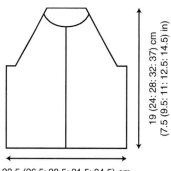

23.5 (26.5: 28.5: 31.5: 34.5) cm
(9.5 (10.5: 11: 12.5: 13.5) in)

19 (24: 28: 32: 37) cm
(7.5 (9.5: 11: 12.5: 14.5) in)

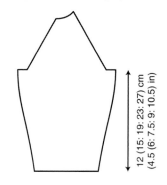

12 (15: 19: 23: 27) cm
(4.5 (6: 7.5: 9: 10.5) in)

SWEETEN

YARN

	1st	2nd	3rd	4th	5th	size
	months		years			
To fit age	0-6	6-12	1-2	2-3	4-5	
To fit chest	41	46	51	56	61	cm
	16	18	20	22	24	in
Rowan 4 ply Soft						
	2	3	3	4	5 x 50gm	

(photographed in Daydream 378)

NEEDLES

1 pair 2¾mm (no 12) (US 2) needles
1 pair 3¼mm (no 10) (US 3) needles

RIBBON TRIM (optional) – 1.20 m of satin bias ribbon

TENSION

28 sts and 36 rows to 10 cm measured over stocking stitch using 3¼mm (US 3) needles.

BACK

Cast on 63 (71: 79: 87: 95) sts using 2¾mm (US 2) needles.

Work in garter st for 3 rows, end with a RS row.

Row 4 (WS): K1, ★P1, K1, rep from ★ to end.

Row 5: As row 4.

Rows 4 and 5 form moss st.

Work in moss st for a further 2 rows, ending with a RS row.

Change to 3¼mm (US 3) needles.

Beg with a P row, work in st st until back measures 11 (14: 17: 20: 24) cm, ending with a WS row.

Shape armholes

Cast off 4 sts at beg of next 2 rows.

55 (63: 71: 79: 87) sts.

Cont straight until armhole measures 11 (12: 13: 14: 15) cm, ending with a WS row.

Shape shoulders and back neck

Cast off 6 (7: 8: 9: 10) sts at beg of next 2 rows.

43 (49: 55: 61: 67) sts.

Next row (RS): Cast off 6 (7: 8: 9: 10) sts, K until there are 10 (11: 12: 13: 14) sts on right needle and turn, leaving rem sts on a holder.

Work each side of neck separately.

Cast off 4 sts at beg of next row.

Cast off rem 6 (7: 8: 9: 10) sts.

With RS facing, rejoin yarn to rem sts, cast off centre 11 (13: 15: 17: 19) sts, K to end.
Complete to match first side, reversing shapings.

LEFT FRONT

Cast on 57 (65: 73: 81: 89) sts using 2¾mm (US 2) needles.
Work in garter st for 3 rows, ending with a RS row.
Work in moss st as given for back for 4 rows, ending with a RS row.
Change to 3¼mm (US 3) needles.
Next row (WS): K1, P1, K1, P to end.
Next row: K to last 2 sts, P1, K1.
These 2 rows set the sts – front opening edge 3 sts in moss st with all other sts in st st.
Cont as set until 3 rows less have been worked than on back to beg of armhole shaping, ending with a RS row.

Shape front slope
Cast off 4 (4: 4: 4: 5) sts at beg of next row, and 3 (4: 4: 4: 4) sts at beg of foll alt row.
50 (57: 65: 73: 80) sts.

Shape armhole
Cast off 4 sts at beg of next row, 3 (3: 4: 4: 4) sts at beg of foll row, then 3 (3: 3: 4: 4) sts at beg of foll alt row. 40 (47: 54: 61: 68) sts.
Dec 1 st at front slope edge of next 15 (21: 25: 29: 33) rows, then on every foll alt row until 18 (21: 24: 27: 30) sts rem.
Cont straight until left front matches back to start of shoulder shaping, ending with a WS row.

Shape shoulder
Cast off 6 (7: 8: 9: 10) sts at beg of next and foll alt row.
Work 1 row.
Cast off rem 6 (7: 8: 9: 10) sts.

RIGHT FRONT

Cast on 57 (65: 73: 81: 89) sts using 2¾mm (US 2) needles.
Work in garter st for 3 rows, ending with a RS row.
Work in moss st as given for back for 4 rows, ending with a RS row.
Change to 3¼mm (US 3) needles.
Next row (WS): P to last 3 sts, K1, P1, K1.
Next row: K1, P1, K to end.
These 2 rows set the sts – front opening edge 3 sts still in moss st with all other sts in st st.
Complete to match left front, reversing shapings.

SLEEVES (both alike)

Cast on 37 (39: 41: 43: 45) sts using 2¾mm (US 2) needles.
Work in garter st for 3 rows, ending with a RS row.
Work in moss st as given for back for 4 rows, inc 1 st at each end of 2nd of these rows and ending with a RS row. 39 (41: 43: 45: 47) sts.
Change to 3¼mm (US 3) needles.
Beg with a P row, cont in st st, shaping sides by inc 1 st at each end of 2nd (2nd: 2nd: 4th: 4th) and every foll 4th (4th: 4th: 6th: 6th) row to 49 (57: 69: 55: 63) sts, then on every foll alt (alt: alt: 4th: 4th) row until there are 61 (67: 73: 79: 85) sts.
Cont straight until sleeve measures 13 (16: 20: 26: 30) cm, ending with a WS row.
Cast off.

MAKING UP

PRESS as described on the information page.
Join both shoulder seams using back stitch, or mattress st if preferred.

Front band
With RS facing and using 2¾mm (US 2) needles, starting and ending at front opening edges,

pick up and knit 44 (48: 52: 56: 60) sts up right front slope to shoulder, 19 (21: 23: 25: 27) sts from back, then 44 (48: 52: 56: 60) sts down left front slope. 107 (117: 127: 137: 147) sts.
Work in moss st as given for back for 3 rows.
Work in garter st for 3 rows.
Cast off knitwise (on WS).
See information page for finishing instructions, leaving a small opening in one side seam to thread ribbon tie through and setting in sleeves using the square set-in method.

Ribbon trim (optional)
Positioning centre of bias ribbon at centre back neck, bind front slope and back neck edges, extending binding to form ties at front opening edges.
Note: If you prefer not to include the ribbon trim, make button loops at ends of front band and attach buttons to side seams to correspond.

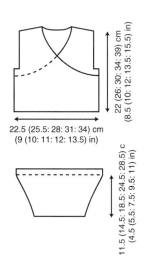

22.5 (25.5: 28: 31: 34) cm
(9 (10: 11: 12: 13.5) in)

22 (26: 30: 34: 39) cm
(8.5 (10: 12: 13.5: 15.5) in)

11.5 (14.5: 18.5: 24.5: 28.5) c
(4.5 (5.5: 7.5: 9.5: 11) in)

DESIGN NUMBER 28

TRANQUIL

YARN

	1st	2nd size	
To fit age	0-6	6-12	months
To fit chest	41	46	cm
	16	18	in

Rowan 4 ply Soft and Kidsilk Haze

			1st	2nd	
A	*KSH	Dewberry 600	1	1	x 25gm
B	4 ply	Daydream 378	1	1	x 50gm

*Use Kidsilk Haze DOUBLE throughout

NEEDLES

1 pair 2¼mm (no 13) (US 1) needles
1 pair 3mm (no 11) (US 2/3) needles

TENSION

30 sts and 38 rows to 10 cm measured over stocking stitch using 3mm (US 2/3) needles.

BOOTEE (make 2)

Cast on 169 (193) sts using 3mm (US 2/3) needles and yarn A DOUBLE.
Break off yarn A and complete bootee using yarn B.

Row 1 (RS of cuff, WS of foot): K1, *K2, lift first of these 2 sts over 2nd st and off right needle, rep from * to end.
Row 2: P1, *P2tog, rep from * to end.
43 (49) sts.
Beg with a K row, work in st st for 12 rows.
Change to 2¼mm (US 1) needles.
Next row (RS): K1, *P1, K1, rep from * to end.
Next row: P1, *K1, P1, rep from * to end.
These 2 rows form rib.
Work in rib for a further 8 (10) rows.
Change to 3mm (US 2/3) needles.
Work in rib for 1 row more, dec 1 st at end of row and ending with RS of foot facing for next row. 42 (48) sts.

Shape instep
Row 1 (RS): (K1, P1) 7 (8) times, K14 (16) and turn.
Row 2: P14 (16) and turn.
Beg with a K row, cont in st st on these 14 (16) sts only for 18 (20) rows.
Break yarn.

Shape foot
With RS facing, rejoin at base of instep and pick up and knit 14 (16) sts up first side of instep, K14 (16) instep sts, then pick up and knit 14 (16) sts down second side of instep, (K1, P1) to end. 70 (80) sts.
Next row (WS): *P1, K1, rep from * to end.
Next row: *K1, P1, rep from * to end.
These 2 rows form moss st.
Work in moss st for a further 13 (15) rows, ending with a WS row.

Shape sole
Row 1 (RS): Work 2 tog, moss st 26 (30) sts, sl 1, K2tog, psso, moss st 8 (10) sts, sl 1, K2tog, psso, moss st 26 (30) sts, work 2 tog.
Row 2: Moss st to end.
Row 3: Work 2 tog, moss st to last 2 sts, work 2 tog.
Row 4: Moss st to end.
Row 5: Work 2 tog, moss st 23 (27) sts, sl 1, K2tog, psso, moss st 6 (8) sts, sl 1, K2tog, psso, moss st 23 (27) sts, work 2 tog.
56 (66) sts.
Row 6: Moss st 28 (33) sts and turn.
Folding bootee with RS facing and using a spare 3mm (US 2/3) needle, cast off all sts together by taking one st from each needle.
Join back seam, reversing seam for turn-back.

DOCKER

YARN

	1st	2nd	size
To fit age	0-6	6-12	months
To fit chest	41	46	cm
	16	18	in

Rowan Wool Cotton

A Inky	908	1	1	x	50gm
B Misty	903	1	1	x	50gm

NEEDLES

1 pair 3mm (no 11) (US 2/3) needles
1 pair 3¾mm (no 9) (US 5) needles

TENSION

23 sts and 32 rows to 10 cm measured over stocking stitch using 3¾mm (US 5) needles.

BOOTEE (make 2)

Cast on 30 (34) sts using 3¾mm (US 5) needles and yarn A.

Row 1 (RS of turn-back, WS of foot): K2, *P2, K2, rep from * to end.

Row 2: P2, *K2, P2, rep from * to end.

These 2 rows form rib.

Work in rib for a further 10 rows.

Change to 3mm (US 2/3) needles.

Work in rib for a further 8 (10) rows.

Change to 3¾mm (US 5) needles.

Work in rib for 1 row more, dec 0 (1) st at end of row and ending with RS of foot facing for next row. 30 (33) sts.

Shape instep

Row 1 (RS): K20 (22) and turn.

Row 2: P10 (11) and turn.

Join in yarn B.

Beg with a K row, work in st st on these 10 (11) sts only as folls:

Using yarn B, work 2 rows.

Using yarn A, work 2 rows.

Rep last 4 rows twice more, then first 0 (2) of these rows again. Break yarn.

Shape foot

With RS facing, rejoin yarn A at base of instep and pick up and knit 10 (11) sts up first side of instep, K10 (11) instep sts, then pick up and knit 10 (11) sts down second side of instep, K to end. 50 (55) sts.

Work in garter st for 9 (11) rows, ending with a WS row.

Shape sole

Row 1 (RS): K2tog, K20 (21), K2tog, K2 (5), K2tog tbl, K20 (21), K2tog tbl.

Row 2: Knit.

Row 3: K2tog, K18 (20), K2tog, K2 (3), K2tog tbl, K18 (20), K2tog tbl.

Row 4: Knit.

Row 5: K2tog, K16 (19), K2tog, K2 (1), K2tog tbl, K16 (19), K2tog tbl. 38 (43) sts.

Row 6: K19 (20), (K2tog) 0 (1) times and turn.

Folding bootee with RS facing and using a spare 3¾mm (US 5) needle, cast off all sts together by taking one st from each needle.

Join back seam, reversing seam for turn-back.

STREAMER

YARN

	1st	2nd	3rd	4th	5th	size
	months		years			
To fit age	0-6	6-12	1-2	2-3	4-5	
To fit chest	41	46	51	56	61	cm
	16	18	20	22	24	in

Rowan 4 ply Soft

A Marine	380	3	3	4	5	5	x	50gm
B Nippy	376	1	1	1	1	1	x	50gm
C Honk	374	1	1	1	1	1	x	50gm

NEEDLES

1 pair 2¾mm (no 12) (US 2) needles
1 pair 3¼mm (no 10) (US 3) needles

TENSION

28 sts and 36 rows to 10 cm measured over stocking stitch using 3¼mm (US 3) needles.

BACK

Cast on 73 (81: 89: 97: 105) sts using 2¾mm (US 2) needles and yarn B.

Rows 1 and 2: Using yarn B, knit.

Join in yarn C.

Rows 3 and 4: Using yarn C, knit.

Change to 3¼mm (US 3) needles.

Row 5: Using yarn B, knit.

Row 6: Using yarn B, purl.

Row 7: Using yarn C, knit.

Row 8: Using yarn C, purl.

Rep rows 5 to 8, once more, then rows 5 and 6 again, ending with a WS row.

Break off yarn B and C and join in yarn A.

Beg with a K row, cont in st st until back measures 14 (17: 20: 23: 27) cm, ending with a WS row.

Shape armholes

Cast off 6 sts at beg of next 2 rows.

61 (69: 77: 85: 93) sts.

Cont straight until armhole measures 12 (13: 14: 15: 16) cm, ending with a WS row.

Shape shoulders and back neck

Cast off 4 (5: 6: 7: 8) sts at beg of next 2 rows. 53 (59: 65: 71: 77) sts.

Next row (RS): Cast off 4 (5: 6: 7: 8) sts, K until there are 9 (10: 11: 12: 13) sts on right needle and turn, leaving rem sts on a holder.

Work each side of neck separately.

Cast off 4 sts at beg of next row.

Cast off rem 5 (6: 7: 8: 9) sts.

With RS facing, rejoin yarn to rem sts, cast off centre 27 (29: 31: 33: 35) sts, K to end.

Complete to match first side, reversing shapings.

FRONT

Work as given for back until front measures 4.5 (8: 11: 14: 18) cm, ending with a WS row.

Place chart

Using the **intarsia** method as described on the information page, place chart as folls:

Next row (RS): K16 (20: 24: 28: 32), work next 42 sts as row 1 of chart, K to end.

Next row: P15 (19: 23: 27: 31), work next 42 sts as row 2 of chart, P to end.

These 2 rows set position of chart.

Keeping chart correct, cont straight until front matches back to beg of armhole shaping, ending with a WS row.

Shape armholes

Cast off 6 sts at beg of next 2 rows.

61 (69: 77: 85: 93) sts.

Cont straight until all 61 rows of chart have been completed, ending with a RS row.

Beg with a P row and using yarn A only, cont

Key ■ A □ B

straight until 12 (12: 14: 14: 14) rows less have been worked than on back to start of shoulder shaping, ending with a WS row.

Shape neck

Next row (RS): K21 (24: 28: 31: 34) and turn, leaving rem sts on a holder.
Work each side of neck separately.
Dec 1 st at neck edge of next 6 rows, then on foll 2 (2: 3: 3: 3) alt rows.
13 (16: 19: 22: 25) sts.
Work 1 row, ending with a WS row.

Shape shoulder

Cast off 4 (5: 6: 7: 8) sts at beg of next and foll alt row.
Work 1 row. Cast off rem 5 (6: 7: 8: 9) sts.
With RS facing, slip centre 19 (21: 21: 23: 25) sts onto a holder, rejoin yarn to rem sts, K to end.
Complete to match first side, reversing shapings.

SLEEVES (both alike)

Cast on 43 (45: 47: 49: 51) sts using 2¾mm (US 2) needles and yarn B.
Beg with 2 rows using yarn B, work 4 rows in striped garter st as given for back.
Change to 3¼mm (US 3) needles.
Work 10 rows in striped st st as given for back then cont in st st using yarn A only **and at same time** inc 1 st at each end of next and every foll 4th (4th: 4th: 6th: 6th) to 59 (69: 79: 65: 73) sts, then on every foll alt (alt: -: 4th: 4th) row until there are 67 (73: -: 85: 91) sts.
Cont straight until sleeve measures 15 (18: 22: 28: 32) cm, ending with a WS row. Cast off.

MAKING UP

PRESS as described on the information page.
Join right shoulder seam using back stitch, or mattress st if preferred.

Neckband

With RS facing, using 2¾mm (US 2) needles and yarn A, pick up and knit 16 (16: 18: 18: 18) sts down left side of neck, knit across 19 (21: 21: 23: 25) sts from front holder, pick up and knit 16 (16: 18: 18: 18) sts up right side of neck, then 35 (37: 39: 41: 43) sts from back.
86 (90: 96: 100: 104) sts.
Beg with a K row, work in rev st st for 4 rows.
Cast off **loosely** knitwise (on WS).
See information page for finishing instructions, setting in sleeves using the square set-in method.

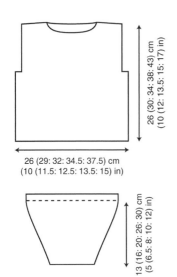

DUMPLING

YARN

	1st	2nd	3rd	4th	5th	size
	months		years			
To fit age	0-6	6-12	1-2	2-3	4-5	
To fit chest	41	46	51	56	61	cm
	16	18	20	22	24	in
Rowan Big Wool						
	2	3	3	4	5	x 100gm

(photographed in Whoosh 014)

NEEDLES

1 pair 12mm (US 17) needles

BUTTONS – 3 x 75317

TENSION

8 sts and 12 rows to 10 cm measured over stocking stitch using 12mm (US 17) needles.

BACK and FRONTS (worked in one piece to armholes)

Cast on 50 (54: 58: 62: 66) sts using 12mm (US 17) needles.
Work in garter st for 3 rows, ending with a **WS** row.
Next row (RS): Knit.
Next row: K3, P to last 3 sts, K3.
These 2 rows set the sts – front opening edge 3 sts in garter st with sts between in st st.
Cont as set until work measures 11 (14: 17: 20: 24) cm, ending with a WS row.

Divide for armholes

Next row (RS): K13 (14: 15: 16: 17) and slip these sts onto a holder for right front, cast off 2 sts, K until there are 20 (22: 24: 26: 28) sts on right needle and slip these sts onto another holder for back, cast off 2 sts, K to end.
Work on this last set of 13 (14: 15: 16: 17) sts only for left front.

Shape left front

Work 1 (3: 3: 3: 3) rows, ending with a WS row.

Shape collar

Row 1 (RS): K to last 3 sts, M1, K3.
14 (15: 16: 17: 18) sts.
Row 2: K4, P to end.
Row 3: Knit.
Row 4: K5, P to end.

Row 5: K to last 6 sts, M1, K6.
15 (16: 17: 18: 19) sts.
Row 6: K7, P to end.
Row 7: Knit.
Row 8: K8, P to end.
Row 9: K to last 8 sts, M1, K8.
16 (17: 18: 19: 20) sts.
Row 10: K9, P to end.
Row 11: Knit.
Row 12: K9 (9: 10: 10: 10), P to end.
Row 13: K to last 9 (9: 10: 10: 10) sts, M1, K to end. 17 (18: 19: 20: 21) sts.
Row 14: K10 (10: 11: 11: 11), P to end.

4th and 5th sizes only

Row 15: Knit.
Row 16: K- (-: -: 11: 12), P to end.

All sizes

Shape shoulder

Next row (RS): K7 (8: 8: 9: 9) and slip these sts onto a holder for left shoulder seam, K to end.
10 (10: 11: 11: 12) sts.
Work in garter st for a further 11 (11: 13: 13: 15) rows for left collar.
Break yarn and leave these sts on another holder.

Shape right front

With **WS** facing, rejoin yarn to 13 (14: 15: 16: 17) sts left on holder for right front and work 1 (3: 3: 3: 3) rows, ending with a WS row.

Shape collar

Row 1 (RS): K3, M1, K to end.
14 (15: 16: 17: 18) sts.
Row 2: P to last 4 sts, K4.
Row 3: Knit.
Row 4: P to last 5 sts, K5.
Row 5: K6, M1, K to end.
15 (16: 17: 18: 19) sts.
Row 6: P to last 7 sts, K7.
Row 7: Knit.
Row 8: P to last 8 sts, K8.
Row 9: K8, M1, K to end.
16 (17: 18: 19: 20) sts.
Row 10: P to last 9 sts, K9.
Row 11: Knit.
Row 12: P to last 9 (9: 10: 10: 10) sts, K to end.
Row 13: K9 (9: 10: 10: 10), M1, K to end.
17 (18: 19: 20: 21) sts.
Row 14: P to last 10 (10: 11: 11: 11) sts, K to end.

4th and 5th sizes only

Row 15: Knit.
Row 16: P to last - (-: -: 11: 12) sts, K to end.

All sizes

Shape shoulder

Next row (RS): Knit.
Break yarn and slip last 7 (8: 8: 9: 9) sts onto a holder for right shoulder seam.
With **WS** facing, rejoin yarn to rem 10 (10: 11: 11: 12) sts and work in garter st for a further 11 (11: 13: 13: 15) rows for right collar.
Break yarn and leave these sts on another holder.

Shape back

With **WS** facing, rejoin yarn to 20 (22: 24: 26: 28) sts from holder for back and work 15 (17: 17: 19: 19) rows, ending with a WS row.

Shape shoulders

Next row (RS): Holding fronts against back with WS together, cast off first 7 (8: 8: 9: 9) sts of back tog with 7 (8: 8: 9: 9) sts of right front to form right shoulder seam, cast off next 6 (6: 8: 8: 10) sts for back neck, then cast off rem 7 (8: 8: 9: 9) sts of back tog with 7 (8: 8: 9: 9) sts of left front to form left shoulder seam.

Cast on 13 (15: 15: 17: 17) sts using 12mm (US 17) needles.

Work in garter st for 3 rows, ending with a **WS** row.

Beg with a K row, cont in st st, shaping sides by inc 1 st at each end of next and every foll alt (alt: 4th: 6th: 8th) row to 19 (19: 19: 23: 25) sts, then on every foll 4th (4th: 6th: 8th: -) row until there are 21 (23: 23: 25: -) sts.

Work a further 3 (5: 5: 7: 9) rows, ending with a WS row. (Sleeve should measure approx 12 (16: 21: 26: 31) cm.) Cast off.

MAKING UP

PRESS as described on the information page. Join collar seam by knitting sts tog in same way as for shoulder seams, then sew one edge of collar to back neck. Join sleeve seams. Insert sleeves into armholes using the square set-in method. Attach buttons to one front opening edge, positioning top button just below start of collar shaping, lowest button 1.5 cm up from cast-on edge, and 3rd button halfway between. Enlarge sts of other front border to form buttonholes.

See information page for finishing instructions.

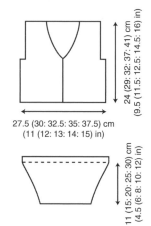

27.5 (30: 32.5: 35: 37.5) cm
(11 (12: 13: 14: 15) in)

24 (29: 32: 37: 41) cm
(9.5 (11.5: 12.5: 14.5: 16) in)

11 (15: 20: 25: 30) cm
(4.5 (6: 8: 10: 12) in)

DESIGN NUMBER 32

RUPERT

YARN

Rowan Wool Cotton

		S/M	M/L		
A Clear	941	2	3	x	50gm
B Antique	900	2	3	x	50gm

NEEDLES

1 pair 3¾mm (no 9) (US 5) needles

TENSION

22 sts and 40 rows to 10 cm measured over garter stitch using 3¾mm (US 5) needles.

MEASUREMENTS

Finished scarf measures 15 (17) cm, 6 (6½) in, wide and 90 (105) cm, 35½ (41½) in, long excluding fringe.

SCARF

Cast on 32 (38) sts using 3¾mm (US 5) needles and yarn A.

Work in garter st for 30 rows, ending with a WS row.

Break off yarn A and join in yarn B.

Work in garter st for 30 rows, ending with a WS row.

Rep last 60 rows 5 (6) times more.

Cast off.

Cut 17 cm lengths of yarn A and yarn B.

Making 5 (6) large knots evenly spaced across ends, knot groups of 8 of these lengths through appropriate coloured end of scarf to form fringe.

INFORMATION PAGE

TENSION

Obtaining the correct tension is perhaps the single factor which can make the difference between a successful garment and a disastrous one. It controls both the shape and size of an article, so any variation, however slight, can distort the finished look of the garment. No-one wants to spend hours and hours making a "skinny rib" when they really want a "sloppy Joe".

Within each pattern there may be different tensions given, for instance, if either **Intarsia** or **Fairisle** techniques **and stocking stitch** are used in the same design. We strongly advise that you knit a square in pattern and or stocking stitch (depending on the pattern instruction) of perhaps 5 - 10 more stitches and 5 - 10 more rows than those given in the tension note. Place the finished square on a flat surface and measure the central area. If you have too many stitches to 10cm try again using thicker needles, if you have too few stitches to 10cm try again using finer needles. Once you have achieved the correct tension your garment will be knitted to the measurements given in the pattern.

SIZE NOTE

The instructions are given for the smallest size. Where they vary, work the figures in brackets for the larger sizes. One set of figures refers to all sizes. For ease in reading charts it may be helpful to have the chart enlarged at a printers and then to outline the size you intend to knit on the chart.

CHART NOTE

Many of the patterns in the book are worked from charts. Each square on a chart represents a stitch and each line of squares a row of knitting. When working from the charts, read odd rows (K) from right to left and even rows (P) from left to right, unless otherwise stated. Each colour used is given a different symbol or letter and these are shown in the **materials** section, or in the **key** alongside the chart of each pattern.

KNITTING WITH COLOUR

There are two main methods of working colour into a knitted fabric: **Intarsia** and **Fairisle** techniques. The first method produces a single thickness of fabric and is usually used where a colour is only required in a particular area of a row and does not form a repeating pattern across the row, as in the fairisle technique.

Intarsia: The simplest way to do this is to cut short lengths of yarn for each motif or block

of colour used in a row. Then joining in the various colours at the appropriate point on the row, link one colour to the next by twisting them around each other where they meet on the wrong side to avoid gaps. All ends can then either be darned along the colour join lines, as each motif is completed or then can be "knitted-in" to the fabric of the knitting as each colour is worked into the pattern. This is done in much the same way as "weaving-in" yarns when working the Fairisle technique and does save time darning-in ends. It is essential that the tension is noted for **Intarsia** as this may vary from the stocking stitch if both are used in the same pattern.

Fairisle type knitting: When two or three colours are worked repeatedly across a row, strand the yarn **not** in use loosely behind the stitches being worked. If you are working with more than two colours, treat the "floating" yarns as if they were one yarn and always spread the stitches to their correct width to keep them elastic. It is advisable not to carry the stranded or "floating" yarns over more than three stitches at a time, but to weave them under and over the colour you are working. The "floating" yarns are therefore caught at the back of the work.

ALL ribs should be knitted to a firm tension, for some knitters it may be necessary to use a smaller needle. In order to prevent sagging in cuffs and welts we suggest you use a "knitting-in" elastic.

PRESSING

After working for hours knitting a garment, it seems a great pity that many garments are spoiled because so little care is taken in the pressing and finishing. After darning in all the ends, block each piece of knitting. Press each piece, except ribs, gently, using a warm iron over a damp cloth. Take special care to press the edges as this will make the sewing up both easier and neater.

FINISHING INSTRUCTIONS

When stitching the pieces together match the colour patterns very carefully. Use a back stitch for all main knitting seams and an edge to edge stitch for all ribs unless otherwise stated.

Join left shoulder seam using back stitch and neckband seam (where appropriate) using an edge to edge stitch.

Sleeves

Set-in sleeves: Set in sleeve easing sleeve head into armhole using back stitch.

Square set-in sleeve: Set sleeve head into armhole, the straight sides at top of sleeve to form a neat right-angle to cast off sts at armhole on back and front, using back stitch.

Shallow set-in sleeves: Join cast-off sts at beg of armhole shaping to cast-off sts at start of sleeve-head shaping. Sew sleeve-head into armhole, easing in shapings.

Join side and sleeve seams using back stitch.

Slip stitch pocket edgings and linings into place.

Sew on buttons to correspond with button-holes.

After sewing up, press seams and hems. Ribbed welts and neckbands and any areas of garter stitch should not be pressed.

 = Easy, straight forward knitting

 = Suitable for the average knitter

 = For the more experienced knitter

ABBREVIATIONS

K	knit
P	purl
st(s)	stitch(es)
inc	increas(e)(ing)
dec	decreas(e)(ing)
st st	stocking stitch (1 row K, 1 row P)
garter st	garter stitch (K every row)
beg	begin(ning)
foll	following
rem	remain(ing)
rev	revers(e)(ing)
rep	repeat
alt	alternate
cont	continue
patt	pattern
tog	together
mm	millimetres
cm	centimetres
in(s)	inch(es)
RS	right side
WS	wrong side
sl1	slip one stitch
psso	pass slipped stitch over
tbl	through back of loop
M1	make one stitch by picking up horizontal loop before next stitch and knitting into back of it
yfwd	yarn forward
yrn	yarn round needle
yon	yarn over needle
yfrn	yarn forward and round needle

ROWAN OVERSEAS DISTRIBUTORS

AUSTRALIA
Australian Country Spinners
314 Albert Street,
Brunswick
Victoria 3056.
Tel: (03) 9380 3888

BELGIUM
Pavan
Koningin Astridlaan 78,
B9000 Gent
Tel: (32) 9 221 8594

CANADA
Diamond Yarn
9697 St Laurent,
Montreal
Quebec H3L 2N1
Tel: (514) 388 6188
www.diamondyarns.com

Diamond Yarn (Toronto)
155 Martin Ross,
Unit 3
Toronto,
Ontario M3J 2L9
Tel: (416) 736 6111
www.diamondyarns.com

DENMARK
Individual stockists -
please contact Rowan for details

FRANCE
Elle Tricot
8 Rue du Coq
67000 Strasbourg
Tel: (33) 3 88 23 03 13
www.elletricote.com

GERMANY
Wolle & Design
Wolfshovener Strasse 76
52428 Julich-Stetternich
Tel : (49) 2461 54735.
www.wolleundesign.de

HOLLAND
de Afstap
Oude Leliestraat 12
1015 AW Amsterdam
Tel : (31) 20 6231445

HONG KONG
East Unity Co Ltd
Unit B2
7/F, Block B
Kailey Industrial Centre
12 Fung Yip Street
Chai Wan
Tel : (852) 2869 7110.

ICELAND
Storkurinn
Kjorgardi
Laugavegi 59
Reykjavik
Tel: (354) 551 82 58

JAPAN
Puppy Co Ltd
TOC Building
7-22-17 Nishigotanda
Shinagwa-Ku
Tokyo
Tel : (81) 3 3494 2395

NEW ZEALAND
Individual stockists -
please contact Rowan for details

NORWAY
Pa Pinne
Tennisun 3D
0777 OSLO
Tel: (47) 909 62 818
www.paapinne.no

SWEDEN
Wincent
Norrtulsgaten 65
11345 Stockholm
Tel: (46) 8 673 70 60

U.S.A.
Rowan USA
4 Townsend West
Suite 8
Nashua
New Hampshire 03063
Tel: (1 603) 886 5041/5043